More Praise for *Career Forward*

"With *Career Forward*, you'll be able to level the playing field and chart a clear path forward. Inspiring, the book provides concrete tools to aid you in your journey, including well-timed wit that will disarm the opposition. Plus, the presentation is always captivating—seriously."

—Jennifer Aaker,
professor, Stanford Graduate School of Business,
and coauthor of *Humor, Seriously*

"Engaging, practical, and hands-on with actionable insights you can put to work right away. No matter where you are on the career ladder, you'll be able to find yourself in this book. Key to *Career Forward*'s appeal is the warmth and genuineness of the authors who seem to be extending themselves to be your personal guides. Don't miss the opportunity to absorb the lessons these two amazing women have to share."

—Carrie Cox, chairman of the board, Organon,
and ranked by *Fortune* for six years as
"One of the Most Powerful Women in Business"

"[Will] make you the first chosen when opportunity knocks. A must read."

—Carol Tomé, CEO of UPS

CAREER FORWARD

Strategies from Women Who've Made It

Grace Puma and
Christiana Smith Shi

Scribner

New York London Toronto Sydney New Delhi

Scribner
An Imprint of Simon & Schuster, LLC
1230 Avenue of the Americas
New York, NY 10020

First Scribner hardcover edition February 2024

SCRIBNER and design are trademarks of Simon & Schuster, LLC

Simon & Schuster: Celebrating 100 Years of Publishing in 2024

For information about special discounts for bulk purchases, please contact Simon & Schuster Special Sales at 1-866-506-1949 or business@simonandschuster.com.

The Simon & Schuster Speakers Bureau can bring authors to your live event. For more information or to book an event, contact the Simon & Schuster Speakers Bureau at 1-866-248-3049 or visit our website at www.simonspeakers.com.

Interior design by Silverglass

Manufactured in the United States of America

10 9 8 7 6 5 4 3 2 1

Library of Congress Cataloging-in-Publication Data has been applied for.

ISBN 978-1-6680-1860-6
ISBN 978-1-6680-1868-2 (ebook)

GRACE

To my husband, Anton, who is one of the greatest blessings in my life, always bringing humor, perspective, and unwavering love to our days.

Also, to my daughter, Annemarie, and son, Joe, who encouraged me to take on the big roles and cheered me on along the way!

CHRISTIANA

To the two people who helped me thrive as a professional and working mom: my mother, Peggyanne Gustafson Smith, PhD, who raised five children and launched a successful career in her forties; and my son, Tim, who was a source of inspiration and love, along with (unfiltered as only children can provide) performance feedback.

Contents

7

What Makes You Special? 99

8

Your 360-Degree Life 113

9

Lucky Like a Duck 133

10

Facing the Forks in the Road 147

11

Shaping Your Leadership Identity 159

12

Own Your Ambition 177

13

Meet the Moment 195

14

It's Worth It 211

Introduction

At the Top of Your Game

Christiana was about to walk onto the stage at Tiger Woods Conference Center, Nike's largest auditorium, when she paused and took a breath. This would be her first town hall meeting as the new president in charge of Nike's direct-to-consumer business, including Nike's stores, e-commerce, and franchise operations—a $4 billion business with over 25,000 employees worldwide. She could see from backstage that the house was packed. There were almost a thousand employees in the hall, with many thousands more watching via livestream. It was the largest audience she'd ever faced, and she knew she needed to inspire, energize, and engage every single person. The event truly underscored the significance of the promotion she'd just earned and how far she'd come as a leader. She had a sudden flashback: for a moment she was that girl from San Diego with a pronounced lisp, whose throat would close up and mouth would go dry when she had to speak in front of a group. Her anxiety about public speaking had been so severe that early in her career she'd avoided making presentations when she could. She was happy to let her colleagues bask in the spotlight.

When Christiana started business school after working for a few years, she realized she needed to vanquish her phobia about public speaking. She quickly discovered that half her grade was going to be based on participation in class discussions. If she didn't get comfortable speaking up regularly in front of ninety students and a professor, she'd likely fail the program. It was a long journey of development, but she was ultimately able to become a dynamic, confident presenter. Now, standing on the big stage, she continued her mental journey into the past, briefly revisiting all the presentation classes she'd taken, the hours of rehearsing before high-stakes meetings, and the coaching sessions that helped her manage her presentation anxiety. She felt supremely comfortable, aware of all the effort and commitment that had led to this point, and excited about stepping onstage. As she walked out to the podium and was greeted by enthusiastic applause, she not only reveled in the moment but *knew* she'd earned it.

The two of us have learned to celebrate such moments in our careers, to feel the gratification of jobs well done and be secure in our achievements. We've built long and satisfying careers that have reaped countless benefits, and we want to share the lessons we've learned, whether you're just starting out or are in mid-career.

People ask us, "How can I get to where *you* are?" Those asking are usually early- or mid-career women who've heard us speak at conferences or have met us through mutual connections. We know they aren't asking the question literally, but rather are looking for guidance in navigating successful careers in an era when there still aren't enough women in senior roles. We're drawn to the idea of exploring in more depth how any woman pursuing a professional path can achieve not just success but fulfillment and joy.

There's no one-size-fits-all answer for everyone. We're strong believers in the power of women charting their own paths based on their unique gifts and aspirations. But we can share a basic mindset that you can use to personalize your path. That mindset is Career Forward—the framework of this book. The Career Forward mindset serves as a blueprint for the choices you make over time that will set you up to thrive in the long term.

If you're always looking ahead, planning your next move, and dreaming about what could be possible, we know exactly how you feel. When you find the right career, work is exciting. It clarifies your passions and talents. A job becomes more than just a paycheck. It's a way to find a sense of fulfillment and purpose, challenge yourself, and make meaningful connections with others who share your interests.

As you progress along your career path and gain knowledge, you'll want to keep increasing your responsibilities. Old tasks become rote, whereas new opportunities engage your curiosity and present a fresh sense of adventure. Whatever your chosen career, if you want to continue to succeed, you'll need to climb the career ladder.

But for women, career advancement can be complicated. The long hours and myriad responsibilities of senior-level roles often create priorities that compete with living a fulfilling life outside the office—including raising a family. Additionally, many studies have shown that women must work harder than men to achieve the same levels of success.[1] This is changing, as more women advance, but it's not happening fast enough. Although there are more women in leadership roles than ever before, and the gender pay gap is slowly narrowing, women still find it more difficult to advance in their careers than men do.

If you're like us, you know that the pursuit of your career passions won't always be an easy road to travel—but that doesn't mean you want to turn around and go back. We reached the top levels of the business world, and we got there while raising kids and juggling family responsibilities. We had to learn a lot of lessons the hard way. When we were coming up in the business world, there just weren't many female leaders whom we could look up to and learn from. We worked through tricky situations with no road map to follow, and had to learn by trial and error. We followed completely different paths to become senior executives, yet we discovered the same underlying truths about getting ahead.

Times have changed radically since those days and there are many more women in leadership roles, but it's surprising and a bit disheartening how much is still the same as it was decades ago. To navigate, women need a career GPS. That means not just a road map but also corrective advice when you make a wrong turn.

Our timing is meaningful. For a while we've been wanting to write a book to give back to women coming behind us, but the news about the Great Resignation and women dialing back their professional lives made creating this book feel even more urgent. We believe in taking the long view of your career—making decisions based not just on the immediate horizon but from the perspective of what's going to give you future opportunities, what will boost your earning power, how you can maximize the value of what you do now, and for those who want it, how you can reach top leadership levels. Some of our guidance might be surprising or go against what you've heard about achieving career success. But we didn't get to where we are today by doing what everyone else did. Instead of a single path to the top, there is a multitude of options. We wrote this book to empower you and help you see the options you have in every aspect of your professional life.

The reality is, we need more women at the highest levels of leadership. For all the talk about gender equality, we're not there yet, and we'll lose ground unless more women think about embracing a Career Forward journey.

That said, there is a caveat: the advice in this book works best if you're passionate about your career and committed to performance. Strong commitment is the foundation of the book, and everything is built on that principle. That means you're consistently operating at a level above what's required in your role; you're surpassing expectations and impressing your superiors, peers, clients, and other stakeholders; and people learn to count on you and trust you because you're so good at your job.

We want to be candid with you that this is what's needed for professional success in general, and it's also what's needed to earn the "career currency" to implement the best practices in this book. Being a high performer earns you more options, flexibility, and freedom. All those benefits will help you craft your best possible career.

We can't know your context, the hurdles you've already leapt, or the obstacles in your path. We can't know if you're starting out with a tank only half full or if you're raring to go. But we can tell you that if you strive to be excellent at what you do and adopt the principles of a Career Forward mindset, you'll be in the driver's seat and on track to your best possible career. We look forward to going on this journey with you.

1

We Have Something to Tell You

Whoever you are, whatever you are, start with that.

—Alice Walker

Few experiences are as satisfying as meeting your kindred spirit in the business world, and that's what happened to us. We bonded, as women often do, by recognizing each other's abilities in a high-stakes setting.

As fate would have it, we were both elected to the board of directors of a large retailer at the same time. It was meaningful to be joining a board together as women, and not only that, to see several other women already on this board. Only about 25 percent of board seats in the Russell 3000 (top publicly traded) companies are currently held by women, and only about 10 percent of the top management positions in S&P 1500 companies are held by women.[1] Having worked in corporate leadership for many years at a variety of companies, we were interested in corporate governance, but I don't think either of us expected this board to also be the launching pad for a great friendship and collaboration.

One afternoon, after the board meeting, we decided to have a drink on San Francisco's Fisherman's Wharf and get better acquainted. The more we talked about our experiences, the more we found we had a surprising number of things in common. To start with, we'd both made it to senior leadership roles as women raising families. We swapped stories about how hard it was to travel for work and not always be home to put our kids to bed during the early years of our careers. We discussed what a grind it can be to do well at work, and how rewarding it is to finally get "dream jobs." And of course we talked about what it feels like to be surrounded by men when there are easily just as many intelligent, capable women who could be serving in those same roles.

We were struck by the similarities in our experiences, given that we'd followed dissimilar paths to get where we were. Despite our unique backgrounds, we saw that we'd both tapped into some powerful lessons that could help other women rise to the top in a variety of circumstances. We agreed that we shared a passion to pass these lessons on to help women succeed after us.

Over the next year, we learned even more about each other—professionally, from serving together on the board, and personally, from our budding friendship outside of work. The more we got to know each other, the more we realized how much cumulative advice we were in a position to pass along.

We'd both found ourselves giving advice to our adult children, who were millennials progressing on their own career journeys. We were moms with a passion to transfer our knowledge and insights to our children so they could benefit from our learning curves. Now we thought about extending that mission to the sea of younger professionals on their own journeys. That's where the idea for this book originated. And we agreed that we'd give our readers the straight scoop. That's the kind of conversation that has benefited us the most over the years, and that's the kind of book we wanted to write.

We imagine this book for up-and-coming leaders who have high aspirations for success. These are new generations who are eager to create their own definition of "having it all." They want to enjoy their work and feel good about the companies they work for. They're ambitious and determined to excel and accumulate wealth. But they also define success more broadly than women of previous eras. As they think about cultivating professional opportunity, they aren't just considering themselves. Many have children or plan on having families, so they want jobs that will enable them to be available when their families need them. They're also asking important questions about quality of life and creating career paths that are personally *fulfilling* as well as successful. As *Fortune* magazine noted in an article on attitudes toward work post-pandemic, "Working hard solely for the sake of the company's bottom line doesn't appeal [to this generation]. But working toward a long-held dream or for personal fulfillment does."[2]

While that way of thinking was rare when we were starting out, times have changed radically. Gallup's *Women in America: Work and Life Well-Lived* report found that 45 percent of employed women aspire to become a CEO or earn a position in senior management or leadership. Interestingly, 54 percent of men said the same, which shows a much smaller difference in ambition than conventional ideas about gender and work would suggest.[3] Additionally, women were just as likely as men to say they were extremely or very serious about achieving such a role. Since there are 45 million professional women in the U.S. workforce, it means over 20 million are actively trying to climb the ladder in their chosen fields—whether in business, education, nonprofits, healthcare, or any number of other professions.

Ask yourself: *Is this you?*

If you're reading this book, you're probably more likely to enjoy the view higher on the ladder. And if you want to crush it at work without losing yourself along the way, then you've already answered. We'll show you how to get where you want to go.

Getting to Know Us

Theorists like to promote the idea that there is a certain "type" who excels professionally. We've noticed a lot of typecasting of successful women, which doesn't exist for men, who are always expected to be ambitious. It's very liberating to know that there isn't just one type. Success for women is as varied as women themselves. Certainly that's been true for us.

Christiana, for example, stayed with McKinsey & Company, the global management consulting firm, for twenty-four years, before moving to Nike, Inc. Grace in certain phases of her career was more peripatetic, working for some of the top companies in the world, including (in order) Gillette, Motorola, Kraft Foods, United Airlines, and PepsiCo, and taking on more responsibility with each position. And yet we both ended up in executive leadership and have similar insights, which made us realize that the value of our advice transcends any specific career path. If it was relevant to us separately, it likely applied to a pretty wide range of careers.

In the chapters to come we'll drill down into what we've learned across the decades. First, though, we'd like to tell you a little something about our formative experiences, and how they shaped our individual journeys.

Christiana:

"I was an anomaly—I didn't fit in, so I chose to stand out."

A professor at business school once told me there was research showing that successful women are either only daughters or oldest daughters. I heard the same thing when I worked at McKinsey.

When I heard this, I always said, "Not me. I'm the middle child of five, and I'm the youngest daughter. And all five of us, from the oldest to the youngest, were born in a span of six years. So if those theories and studies are correct, I guess I'm an anomaly." I later realized that in many ways—well beyond birth order—I *was* an anomaly. I always paved my own path.

I was born in Winnetka, Illinois, on the North Shore of Chicago, and spent my first ten years there before my parents moved to San Diego. San Diego was a Navy town at that time, and a relatively isolated place.

My dad was a charismatic man and a natural-born salesman. He could sell sand in the desert. Mom had been a model and a ballet dancer before she got married, and she hadn't finished college. She went back to school when my youngest brother was in kindergarten. Dad got a series of sales jobs after we moved to California, but those were years of struggle. He was laid off during the recession of 1973–74, which coincided with my mother finally getting her bachelor's degree. Her focus was psychology, and her first job after she earned her BS was fielding calls on a suicide hotline, making about $18,000 a year. She never expected to support all seven of us on that salary, but she did—and remained the primary wage earner in our family until all of us kids were out of the house. She kept going to school and earned her master's pretty quickly, then her PhD. She rose from there to become the executive director of an outpatient treatment center for the chronically mentally ill, and ultimately became a senior administrator of mental health programs for San Diego County. My mom's path wasn't straight, it wasn't quick, and it had a lot of setbacks, but her perseverance and ability to excel in her professional life were an inspiration to me.

I figured out early on that I didn't want to stay in San Diego, and I didn't want to constantly struggle to make ends meet. I knew from watching my mom that education was the way out. College became the reset button for me.

There were 800 students in my San Diego high school graduating class, but I was the only one to go to Stanford University, even though it was in-state. My guidance counselor advised against applying to Stanford, telling me the odds were too long to justify the application fee. My parents told me I should go to the local state school, because it would be a lot cheaper. I listened to all this advice, but I also did my own research, which mostly meant reading a lot of college brochures, since Google didn't exist yet, and talking to any local alums I could find. What I learned about Stanford—that it was ranked higher than my local options, had more courses in the fields I liked, and offered the potential for several scholarships—convinced me that it was worth an application. It still took a real leap of faith for me to use the money I earned from after-school jobs to cover the cost of applying. Being admitted to my top-choice university was my first experience aspiring to something important and achieving it even in the face of naysayers.

My primary goal in landing a job after graduating college was just to be able to pay back my student loans. Investment banking and management consulting were the two highest-paying intern programs at the time, so that's where I focused. The big consulting firms turned me down flat because I did poorly on their "case study" interviews—

the ones where you're presented with a difficult business problem and some background information, then asked to come up with recommendations to solve the problem during the interview. It turns out that like so many other skills, handling a case study interview can be practiced until you get good at it, but I didn't learn that until I had a few more years of work experience.

I was very good at math, though, so the banks loved me. I spent my first three years out of college on Wall Street, working for Merrill Lynch. I grew up a lot in those years, learning to stand on my own and be a professional in a pretty unforgiving environment. I closely observed how senior people dressed, talked, worked, and even ate (not having grown up knowing which fork to use at formal dinners). I started to figure out what "my way" was going to look like.

Our intern class, to Merrill's credit, was almost 50 percent women, but in many ways, we were playing by old rules. In a photo memorializing the group, the women are in the front row, with the men standing behind us. We all have silk bow ties straight out of the movie *Working Girl*. We wore skirt suits and jackets every day—no pants allowed. We were women trying to stylistically emulate men, but we were also striving to break away from stereotypes in ways that counted.

Merrill had an initiative that paid for us to pursue our MBAs at night, but it didn't take long for me to realize that if I was serious, adding classwork onto a full workday wouldn't yield the result I wanted. I had to go all in. So, having only enough money to apply to two full-time graduate schools, I chose Stanford and Harvard. Stanford wait-listed me, but Harvard welcomed me to their program. At the time, I thought I was lucky, because I could've easily struck out at both schools and been left with night school as my only option, but I realized later that I created that luck through my track record at school, my performance at work, and my network of supporters who wrote recommendations. In any case, I was off to Cambridge, Massachusetts.

By that time, I knew what I wanted to do. Merrill Lynch was a client of the management consulting firm McKinsey & Company, and while at Merrill, I'd volunteered to be a client team member on a project that McKinsey was doing. The McKinsey people parachuted in, and I was immediately enthralled. They were the smartest people I'd ever met. They were polished. They flew in from Italy, France, London, and Canada, and they all worked together in an instantly collaborative way. It was a very different culture from the one I was used to in investment banking.

I remember thinking, *These are my people.* From then on, it became my goal to join McKinsey, but I had to work for it, including learning how to handle the case study interviews that had stumped me back in college. I started preparing early for each round of McKinsey interviews, focusing on mastering common business problem-solving techniques and developing some "pattern recognition" about the typical solutions that could be applied.

I was eager to return to the West Coast, so the first year at HBS I applied for a summer job in McKinsey's San Francisco office. I thought I interviewed well, but McKinsey turned me down. Later I learned it was largely because McKinsey's San Francisco office was small and they didn't have many summer spots available, but at the time I thought I'd struck out with them yet again. I ended up working for a different consulting firm, which sent me to work at a steel mill in Louisiana. I figured out what management consulting entailed that summer, and I also determined what kind of cultural fit I was looking for. That summer firm definitely wasn't it.

When I got back to Harvard's campus for my second year, McKinsey started calling me, and I realized my summer experience had made me a more attractive hire, even though I hadn't loved it. I kept holding out for McKinsey's San Francisco office, even as I was getting offers from other firms. Looking back, I'm struck by my sense of self—that I could keep holding out for McKinsey until they came up with the offer I wanted. They finally did in January, offering me a job in the city immediately after graduation.

I've discovered many times since then that you may not always know what path to take or when to go or stay. But there are times when you just know what's right in your gut. That was McKinsey for me. Being able to recognize how and when to make those choices is one of the areas we'll explore in this book.

Only 20 percent of my classmates at Harvard Business School were women, so many of the friendships I developed were with men, and they were supportive. When I was honored as a George F. Baker Scholar, which is reserved for those in the top 5 percent academically, I remember how the guys clapped and cheered and said, "We knew you were going to get it." I was beginning to recognize that I had a secret strength—likability— and that it mattered just like hard work mattered. Being the smart woman with the easygoing personality was a benefit, and it was authentic.

I came to see that while IQ is important, emotional intelligence (EQ) can be the difference-maker. One of my closest McKinsey mentors, Bill Meehan, once said to me, "Christiana, never underestimate the value of being someone people want to spend time with." When I asked if he thought I could be that person, he told me it was in my wheelhouse. I embraced that goal and it has benefited me in countless ways over the years—and by the way, I wasn't pretending. The good vibes I gave off were genuine. They used to call me the iron fist in the velvet glove, because I could give very tough feedback, but in a supportive way. I knew that the more senior you become, the more intimidating you are without even opening your mouth. When I was a junior associate, I was scared of the partners—everybody was. So when I became a partner, it was important to me that I not lead by intimidation. I liked being in a position to help shape the culture. And during my entire time at McKinsey, I never stopped appreciating the ways the organization was responsive to change, growth, and diversity.

It was uncommon for senior McKinsey partners to leave for executive roles in corporations. The general wisdom was that if you stayed in consulting too long, you weren't that attractive to other industries. Still, it did happen from time to time. One of my colleagues became CEO of QVC (now Qurate). More recently, a very close McKinsey friend of mine was named CEO of Starbucks. Those partners who migrated to executive roles might have been rare birds, but I took notice. Over the years I'd spent time and effort cultivating relationships with recruiters who called me regularly. I always tried to help them find someone else for jobs I wasn't interested in.

It was part of my fundamental code of networking and being a person who was open and helpful.

A male colleague once told me disapprovingly that I spent too much time helping people in my network connect to opportunities. What he couldn't grasp was how often those relationships would come back to benefit me. We'll talk more about that later, but suffice it to say that those relationships led directly to the opportunity to take on an executive role at Nike after I'd been a senior partner at McKinsey for ten years.

Grace:

"Don't look back. Look forward to new challenges and make the most of them."

My parents came to the United States from Cuba in the early sixties, right after the revolution. My oldest sister was two years old, and my mother was pregnant with my second sister. I wasn't in the picture yet.

My mother and father had been together since she was sixteen—she from a wealthy family and my dad from a working-class family who owned a dry-cleaning business. My father was a great striver with a tremendous work ethic, working in his family business from a young age and attending university in Cuba to become a CPA. After my maternal grandparents lost everything in the revolution, my mother's father was able to get his family out of Cuba through personal friends and contacts, and they came to the United States. They settled in Chicago, where my father obtained a job as an accountant, and they bought a small house with their limited resources. I was born a few years later. I remember my father telling stories about his determination to learn English quickly so he'd be able to work in the United States. He was enormously driven, and clearly the responsibility and pressure of providing for our family sat squarely on his shoulders. His intelligence and drive paid off, and he made his way up to the senior level of a corporation, where he led the finance and supply chain functions.

Once they were in the United States, my parents never looked back. They weren't focused on what they'd lost, but on what they'd gained in coming to America. I never felt for a minute that they possessed any type of victim or entitlement mentality—just gratitude and an intense desire to thrive, which they passed on to their three daughters.

There were many years of struggle to make ends meet. During that time, my aunt came to live with us from Cuba. For my father, it added to the financial pressures of supporting an expanded family in a new country. We had a small three-bedroom ranch home, and we three girls shared one room so our aunt could have her own room.

My dad was the alpha in this family of females. He ruled the roost, and my parents had a very traditional relationship. My mother was a loving and positive person with strong faith. She was accommodating to my father. I remember how every morning until the day he died, she'd lovingly prepare his breakfast and give it to him with his espresso coffee to start his day.

My mother had the full responsibility for taking care of the kids and the home. When I started kindergarten, she also took on a job as a secretary, and for decades she worked and saved her full salary, putting it into retirement investments.

By the time she retired, my parents had built a solid nest egg that allowed them to enjoy a modest and joyful retirement. This fit in with another aspect of a traditional immigrant upbringing—the idea that you can prosper in life if you take advantage of the opportunities that present themselves.

The main attribute that my childhood gifted me with was resilience. As a child I watched my parents struggle to establish themselves in a new country and support their young family. I often saw them under great stress in a high-risk pursuit that sometimes didn't work out the way they'd hoped. In those circumstances, I witnessed their resilience—the way they'd regroup and try something new. Watching them, I internalized the lesson of resilience—which is that no problem I'd encounter in life was too great to be resolved. I didn't dwell on what I didn't have or what the cost of failure could be. I was laser focused on building what I *could* have. I always looked ahead to what I wanted in life and plotted a course to get there. This began at an early age. I can vividly remember being in grade school and a teacher asking me, "How did you get so confident?" I didn't know how to answer that question, but I did know I'd had a strong sense of self since I was little. I'm sure that confidence came from watching my parents start over and build a life together. It wasn't a conscious attitude—just something I picked up from them.

I learned from my parents in general ways, but my aunt was a role model when it came to a career. She completed her business degree and became a successful businesswoman in the financial world, and I wanted to emulate her. I would spend summers with her in New Jersey, soaking up her lifestyle and closely observing the way she lived. Her success was impressive, and I admired her poise and style, and the fact that she was super smart. She loved her career, and it made a big impression on me that she also had a fantastic marriage of equals. She didn't fit the stereotypes of the time. She had a soft side to her and a strong side to her, and she always exuded focus, confidence, and exceptional drive. I looked at her and thought, *I want that.* She was the first woman I knew personally who had a life I could picture myself in.

I also emulated my father's focus on financial security. When you've lost everything, as my parents had, financial security becomes front of mind, and I learned to strive for it. Well into my professional life, my father would caution me, "Grace, you can never save enough money," and his lessons stuck. It wasn't about chasing the gold ring, but I was always focused on being a financially independent woman and aware that financial security creates options. The truth of that was even more obvious when I became a single mother.

My dad was a great supporter of my dreams. He'd always been passionate about his own work, and he relished my success and achievements and never implied there were any boundaries to what I could achieve. He loved watching my career progress. For decades, he would write me letters conveying his learnings and advice told from the viewpoint of three imaginary squirrels (black, gray, and brown). For example:

"The higher in the rank ladder, the more exposure to the storm winds."
"Squirrels never have enough nuts put away for an unexpected long winter."

These letters would arrive serendipitously when I was about to make a big career move or was at a critical decision crossroads. I often reread them to remind myself of the advice he'd shared. He had a very good head for business—he possessed a natural intuitive ability to read and anticipate situations. I inherited some of that ability, and it has served me well.

Shortly after I entered the workforce, after getting married, I moved to Boston to work at a large chemical producer, BASF, and at Gillette. It was in these early jobs that I became aware that my work was important to me, and I wanted to keep learning and doing more. An aspiration mindset set in. I was bold enough to take on the tough jobs, and as I delivered, more opportunities quickly followed. My formula to grow my career was rooted in being 300 percent committed to doing a great job and making an impact quickly while learning more and more in each role. However, I also held on to the idea that I was never *owned* by the companies I worked for. I was loyal and appreciative, but I was never overly attached. That gave me the objectivity to trigger a move or expand a role when I needed to accelerate my career trajectory.

Even early in my career, I put a lot of pressure on myself to master new technical aspects of my job quickly to avoid being vulnerable and to perform at my highest level. I jumped into new areas with both feet by doing research, taking webinars, and peppering my managers and peers with questions. The better I understood key technologies, the higher my confidence. For example, when I first moved to Motorola, I had to learn about the paging and cellular infrastructure technology to be able to effectively negotiate for the parts my team was buying for the company. I wasn't afraid to admit it when I didn't understand something. I always asked for help, and I found that people appreciated that. Not only did I increase my competence, but I also developed strong relationships with my colleagues. Those relationships were just as important as the skills development.

The point of relating our background stories? Certainly, both of us were blessed with supportive families. That isn't a requirement of success in life, but it helps. It's never *enough*, though. Both of us built our careers—as *you* should—from foundations of personal strengths, ambition, opportunity, resilience, and drive. Beyond family, we didn't have many role models when we were starting out, but we can be that for you today. We'd like to help you write a story for yourself that is as rich as possible.

KEY TAKEAWAYS

- Many women aspire to succeed in their careers, but the lack of role models and success stories can hamper progress.

- The principles of career success transcend any particular field or career path.

- Develop your own "career GPS" early on to help you stay on track.

2

Career Forward

Your work is to discover your work and then,
with all your heart, to give yourself to it.
—Buddha

W e're aware that there are plenty of perspectives about what a good career looks like and what people must do to get ahead. But believing that you should pursue salary increases or titles at the expense of managing career goals isn't a smart way to cultivate long-term happiness or well-being. Instead, it's essential to do some soul-searching and identify the factors that are most important for you in a professional role. These might include having financial stability, enjoying a good work/life balance, living in a specific city, feeling positive about your organization's culture, or working in a certain field. These factors help point toward what we call your career "Cardinal Direction" and provide clarity on whether you're on the right path.

We call that being Career Forward, which means to focus on your career path rather than your current job. If you chase the next job title or salary bump, you'll take your eye off the long-range perspective that really leads to success. We don't mean to denigrate the job you have now or say it doesn't matter. It absolutely matters. Being consistently good at your job is the price of admission to advancing your career. But we also believe that being good at your job is not enough, and those who overly focus on job instead of career are likely to get stalled. Career Forward means having such a strong focus on the future that you're always moving in the right direction.

We're addressing this head on right up front because although a Career Forward mentality is a key to success, it's not well understood. We've found that many younger workers, not just women, don't know how to either strategize or operationalize their careers beyond occasionally updating their résumés, scanning open positions, and sporadically networking when they feel dissatisfied or vulnerable in their jobs. Others operate on a blind faith that good work speaks for itself, and they pour themselves into their jobs, assuming a big reward is on the horizon—which isn't necessarily the case. Still others are confident their jobs are secure or think if they just give it time, the raises and promotions will come. They're shattered when this doesn't happen.

All these assumptions are made by talented, hardworking, ambitious young people who are accustomed to excelling at everything they do. But they're stymied by a job-first mindset, which leaves them waiting in the wings, no matter how talented they are.

Career Forward thinking opens up your options, enabling you to seize every opportunity around you to enhance your value and ability to contribute. And in time, that equity can become leverage for pay increases, promotions, flexible work arrangements, and better job offers from other companies.

This is a more nuanced perspective than you're probably used to. We're not saying, "Go flat out all the time. Sacrifice everything for your career." Nor are we suggesting that you be casual about your job. You need to do both, demonstrating commitment in your current position while looking ahead with a Career Forward mindset. We're going to help you find that balance.

We also respect your different aspirations. For some of you, running a company someday is the Holy Grail. (Few women aspired to that goal in earlier eras. Now, in some fields, there are *more* women business owners than men.) Others have different goals—as entrepreneurs or academics, in public service, healthcare, or any number of occupations. No matter what your ambitions, Career Forward will benefit you.

Playing the career long game may feel counterintuitive, especially if you're used to boldly taking a leap whenever there's a tantalizing lead. But we're telling you, as a first step, to stop chasing open jobs and seeking title changes and salary increases as a means of obtaining long-term well-being and success. Begin viewing the landscape in a more strategic way. For example, in the early years, your job and your career can feel very similar as you focus on making enough to live on while establishing yourself. Think of them as overlapping circles. Anything else you get from your job feels like a bonus for your career. Then as you move beyond this entry level, your career and job may diverge into two distinct spheres. If your job is going well, it doesn't automatically mean that your career is moving in a satisfying direction or you're meeting your long-term goals. You need to be alert to the right signs.

We've both seen career stagnancy happen to people. Christiana can remember working with a teammate at one of her first temp jobs in the jewelry department of a large retailer. This woman had been there for five years already and was frustrated that she was still doing the same clerical job. She told Christiana that she'd focused on keeping her head down and doing the day-to-day work, but that she was now looking up to find herself in a job she wasn't crazy about, with no plans and few options to move ahead. She forgot about tending to her career. As she learned, it's much easier to get stuck than you might think.

This is your career, and you're the one at the wheel. So where do you want to go? You wouldn't just get in your car and start driving without having a clear idea of a destination. The same is true for your career. If you don't actively think about your destination, you'll probably end up somewhere else. You need that "career GPS" to guide you. For a GPS to be helpful though, you need to set it to a specific destination—that's what we call the "Cardinal Direction," or the true north of your career.

Finding Your Cardinal Direction

Most career guides offer similar advice on the topic of finding the right path, exhorting readers to inventory their skills, examine their values, and explore their passions. We generally agree with those ideas but want to take the discussion further in the context of Career Forward.

First, your Cardinal Direction evolves. It grows as you grow. It's not a fixed star, but a living path. Your life experience is a constant process of learning and finding out how you're performing, whom you like to work with, what environment energizes you the most, and so on. All that data helps inform your personal direction. This two-part process of experimentation and reflection is the difference between just having career goals and having a path. Think of it as a repeating dynamic: experiment, reflect; experiment, reflect. This dynamic will help keep you on a steady course.

Let's go back to basics. How do you begin locating the path that's right for you? If you're just graduating from school or are in the early stages of your career, we suggest that you just get a job and use that job as a laboratory for your larger career. Think of yourself as being in a phase of experimentation. Be mindful of what gives you energy, what environments you enjoy, what tasks excite you. Don't be discouraged if your job feels like the wrong fit. Examine those feelings. Identify when you feel unfulfilled or find the work a grind. The experience of a poor fit helps teach us what *does* fit.

If you've been in the workplace for a while and you're at a point where you're trying to figure out the right direction going forward, you can mine the experiences you've already had. Begin that process of experimentation and reflection from your current position.

Grace

I didn't wake up and say I wanted to be a chief operating officer (COO), but I'd discovered during my early career years that I enjoyed working in dynamic situations. I found that I was energized by environments that changed, where I could be involved in transformation. I needed to be able to create something new, and I thrived on fast-paced environments. Those were all things I learned about myself, and they transcended the actual job or industry.

But those qualities were also what attracted me to the procurement field and eventually to supply chain, which involves the flow of purchased materials, manufacturing, and the conversion of those materials into a finished product, as well as distribution to the end user.

I knew I wasn't the only supply chain expert in the world. There were others who'd grown up in operations running the plants, which is a core activity. But I was able to view the landscape from a different perspective and see strategic shifts. I could look around corners and mobilize teams with different types of expertise. These abilities fit with my desire to create transformation and opened doors of opportunity for me.

This process of experimentation and reflection goes on throughout your working life. Most people don't just land on a Cardinal Direction overnight. It grows and develops as they do. One reason is simple: you don't know what you don't know. For example, people usually choose college majors based on vague ideas of what they like to do, what others told them they would be good at, or how they see their future. But according to a 2022 survey by Intelligent.com, more than half of college graduates don't work in their field of study.[1] There are of course various reasons for this, but undoubtedly one reason is the realization that the actual day-to-day of the field doesn't match what they want.

Christiana

My first two summer jobs in college were temp jobs because I needed money more than specific work experience. Still, I learned something about myself from those jobs: I liked being around smart people, I could keep up in fast-paced work environments, and I could jump into new situations and figure out what to do pretty quickly. I realized before my senior year I needed the kind of job I could put on a résumé that would help me find solid employment when I graduated. I applied and got an internship with the federal government. That internship got me interviews with the big banking programs, and that led me to Merrill Lynch. I was attracted to Merrill because they wanted candidates with perfect GPAs, and I was that kid who'd always chased A's in school. I thought I'd be happy there. But when I got into investment banking, I found that while I loved the numbers and the analytics, I hated the culture and the lifestyle. I had to experience it to understand that about myself.

EXERCISE: FIND YOUR CARDINAL DIRECTION

To begin the process, do a self-evaluation in four arenas: environment, subject matter, passion, and purpose.

ENVIRONMENT

You can examine the question of environment on the most granular level. It boils down to the setting where you want to spend your days: indoor, outdoor; large company, small business, solo entrepreneur, protocol heavy, informal; multiple management levels, set hours (nine to five), flexible hours; remote, on-site, or hybrid—and so on. You can also measure the intensity level on a scale from what you'd experience in, say, an emergency room to what you'd experience in a small office. Do the same with the level of risk—from a high-stakes game or a law enforcement mission to a secure tenured position.

The environment is a primary consideration because it's literally the framework of your career life.

SUBJECT MATTER

As a simple exercise, list what you were good at in school: science, creative writing, math, history, computers, art, music, political science, engineering, sociology, etc. This forte might have arisen naturally— the way Christiana was always good at math. Or it might be a skill that you pushed yourself to develop, the way some people learn musical instruments. Being good at something is an automatic bonus, and often it's the same as the thing you enjoy most. That's where passion comes in.

PASSION

Passions expressed in childhood often fade—think of how common it is when we're very young to want to be a firefighter, a ballerina, or a baseball player—but sometimes they endure to form the raw material of the career you end up pursuing. Grace's son always wanted to be a meteorologist—since the age of three he had been enthralled by clouds and weather patterns—and that's the profession he eventually chose. That level of certainty is rare, but you might find clues to your future in the passions of your youth. Maybe you had a fascination with biology and loved studying the habits of animals or bugs. Maybe you imagined yourself on a stage giving speeches. Maybe you always preferred to be in creative environments, drawing, painting, or playing an instrument. Maybe you had an entrepreneurial spirit and loved making and selling things or enjoyed design and marketing. Maybe you wanted to travel the world or help people in struggling countries. If you pull on the threads of your old passions, you might find clues about the kind of work that could engage you today.

PURPOSE

Your career is not just about what you do and how you advance. It's about what drives you—your sense of purpose. This self-identified mission is not an abstraction. It's the engine that drives the actions you take and that keeps your career path from being a vague ideal. People with a high sense of purpose are more likely to be passionately engaged in their work.

According to research by Anthony L. Burrow, Ferris Family Associate Professor of Life Course Studies at Cornell University, "Purpose is a forward-looking directionality, an intention to do something in the world. It's different [from] a goal, which can be accomplished."[2] Purpose, which is integral to the human experience, makes you more effective.

In one study Burrow asked participants to take a survey to determine their level of purpose and also to keep a diary for fourteen to twenty-one days. He reported that those who scored higher on a sense of purpose weren't as emotionally affected by everyday stresses. This outcome has the potential not only to improve health and well-being, but also to make a person more effective in a workplace environment.

Hopefully, you can see why having a Cardinal Direction is a good thing, but at the same time we've learned from experience that being too precise about career goals can backfire. Almost every profession has a gold-standard or "ideal" path. For example, in consulting or law, the goal is to get to partnership, while in academia, the goal is to get to tenure. Some organizations number each level of advancement, and people get caught up in the race to reach higher and higher designations. This is a myopic view of what a successful career can be. In our own careers, we each made unexpected detours that ended up being the perfect roads, taking us to our desired destinations through different routes.

The Benefits of Career Forward

Before we go further, let's talk about the major benefits of Career Forward. They reach into the heart of job satisfaction, independence, and self-worth, which become lifelong advantages.

There are five worth highlighting:

1. A Career Forward mindset reduces your career risk.

When you operate from a Career Forward point of view, you're not beholden to any one job, and that means you're less vulnerable. We all know how fast conditions can change—just consider recent recessions and the pandemic upheaval. One of the great advantages to Career Forward thinking is that you're never tied down to a particular job or industry. You have a built-in safety net and escape clause, having prepared to easily shift gears.

In our careers, we were both always considering what we could do next. How we could contribute more. What new opportunity was going to present itself. We weren't waiting for a crisis to develop and threaten our job security because we were thinking ahead. This view enables you to build up the confidence to make changes without fear and the ability to tolerate some blowback and career storms. Nagging anxiety, which can sidetrack your job performance and satisfaction, is virtually nonexistent in this scenario.

If you have a long-game view, you're thinking about how to continue to advance your career. Have you reached the point where you're not growing anymore? You need to move or shift or change or look for something new. How do you avoid getting attached to your own performance reviews? ("My boss loves me . . . I'm doing great . . . I got top ratings.") Complacency can quickly lead to job insecurity without your recognizing it.

2. A Career Forward approach keeps you in the driver's seat.

With a Career Forward mindset, nobody owns you. Your primary loyalty is to yourself and your own set of career choices. That's not to say you're not dedicated to your job—of course you are. You can thrive in a job and be viewed as a great asset to your company. But you're always keeping an eye on that long view to test where you really stand.

It may surprise you to know that early in our careers, neither of us saw ourselves ending up in top management—and we'd bet that's typical for a lot of women when they are starting out. Over time, though, as you regularly revisit and realign your career goals, you should set your aspirations high. If you don't see many people who look like you in your ideal job, you may have to pave your own path, and that's okay. If you scan the horizon and don't see your ideal job, figure out how you can create it.

As you think about where you want to go in your career, give yourself permission to see the world without limitations and get excited about the many possibilities that are in front of you. As the saying goes, "What would you do if you knew you couldn't fail?" When you bring this attitude and passion to your work, the monetary *and* psychic rewards will follow.

When you choose a career path, don't be afraid to embrace your ambition. This hasn't always been such a comfortable idea for women. In previous decades, there weren't many examples of public women who were praised for their ambition, and unfortunately some of those attitudes linger. We're saying that it's completely okay to be ambitious. You can repurpose what was considered a negative characterization for women into a positive. All ambition means is that you're choosing to run your own show.

3. Career Forward thinking helps you know when to say yes or no.
With a Career Forward mindset, you have a clearer sense of when to say yes and when to say no. Often, early in their careers women tend to say yes too often, wanting to be agreeable. It's easy to be flattered by positive feedback and the perceived sense of being indispensable—but no one is. It's a form of entrapment.

When someone at work is giving you a lot of positive reinforcement, and they're asking you to take additional responsibility or helm a project, the glow of approval can mask the fact that you might not be getting fairly compensated or are being stuck with a thankless job. Career Forward enables you to evaluate whether an opportunity is worthwhile for your journey or not. Should it be a yes or a no for you?

Christiana once counseled a junior colleague who'd been asked to run a big information technology project in her company. This woman had just spent several years moving her career away from being an engineer to being a general manager. Now she was being offered a promotion, but it would put her back in deep tech—with an extremely difficult project to boot. The offer was presented to her as an important promotion with the implication that she couldn't say no.

Christiana talked the decision through with her, emphasizing that the woman should prioritize what she wanted for her career journey. The colleague realized that what she wanted was to run a business, which meant she needed to stay on the general management path, even if it meant leaving her current company. Ultimately, she said no to the technology project, in a professional and collaborative way—and guess what? The company didn't fire her. In fact, she was promoted six months later into a general management role, which was what she'd wanted all along. Knowing when and how to turn down a job that doesn't support your career goals is a key capability for any professional to develop early in their journey.

With Career Forward, you learn to keep your cool and not be flustered by promotion offers that aren't really advancing you, or flattery that's actually the kiss of career death. In the long run, you'll learn it's worth it to say no in those circumstances, even if it means a short-term setback.

4. Career Forward thinking offers a bigger long-term payoff.

When you manage your career, you're less dependent on the judgments of others. Your validation comes from meeting your own interior benchmarks. This in turn leads others to elevate their opinion of your abilities. There's an accepted psychology related to how companies sense when someone is just in it for a job as opposed to having a strong, independent career purpose. Others value you more when they see that you are career oriented. If your colleagues believe that your focus is on growth and progression and on where you want to take your life, your organization will see you differently. The net effect will be that your work life will become more empowering and fulfilling.

Often people with ambition tend to downplay the idea of satisfaction. There's a lot of emphasis on hard knocks. We all know the expression "That's why they pay me the big bucks," referring to the belief that a highly compensated job must be loaded with suffering. But when you're independent and self-motivated, that theory doesn't apply. As we've described, despite our different career paths, we had in common the fact that our work was always very demanding—and we were happy because we made sure it was the right fit.

5. A Career Forward mindset helps you ride the waves.

Career Forward helps you navigate difficulties in the workplace. Having a larger purpose allows you to ride the rough waves, and sometimes even to stay in a job for a time because you need the experience or recognize an eventual payoff.

Certain struggles are a part of every career journey. Being able to evaluate them in a broader context is very empowering. You gain the professional maturity to make these evaluations.

We've both been in jobs that were very hard, dealing with difficult challenges and company turnarounds. In the midst of the tumult, we were also aware that these were great learning experiences. Career Forward enabled us to have that sensibility.

Watch Where You're Going

It's all up to you. What if the prescribed path to success in your profession doesn't seem all that appealing? Maybe you love the work you do, but don't want to travel as much as a job typically requires, or you don't find that the career trajectory or timing offers sufficient flexibility.

Just because you want to go in a direction that is different from what people expect doesn't mean you're about to make a wrong turn. There have been many times in our lives when we've made unorthodox career moves that ended up being perfect for us. Instead of climbing straight up the corporate ladder, most people zig and zag in unexpected ways. Sometimes they arrive at the same goal they originally had but have taken a different route to get there—and sometimes they end up in a totally different spot that fits them even better.

The key is to get crystal clear about what you want out of your career while being mindful of how it will affect your life overall. Then use those choices to set personal "guardrails" on the career decisions and job choices you make. For example, maybe you want to work for a company that has a purpose you feel good about, and you realize that's a non-negotiable for you—no matter how much the job pays. Or you and your family have settled in a certain city, and you don't want to be uprooted unless it's a once-in-a-lifetime offer. These kinds of preferences are unique to you, and they must be among your calculations when you are making important decisions about your career. We believe in taking a more flexible approach to setting your career goals than the typical "Where do you want to be in X years?" type of career planning. These personal guardrails can help you stay on your "right path," even if you change your near-term direction to address a specific life situation or job opportunity.

EXERCISE: SET YOUR GUARDRAILS

Find a time to sit down and evaluate your guardrails— what's most important to you—and then plan on a regularly scheduled checkup, at least every year. Some of what matters to you will probably change as your career advances, but this checkup will help you determine what is non-negotiable, what aspects are nice to have but negotiable, and what's not really on your radar now, but may be important down the road. Once you've completed the exercise, take a look at the total picture and ask yourself how your current job measures up. This can be a wake-up call, particularly if non-negotiables are not being met or too many preferences are unaddressed.

YOUR GUARDRAILS			
	Non-Negotiable	Preferred	Not Crucial... Now
Compensation			
Title			
Industry			
Job impact on company			
Leadership opportunities			
Location			
Work remotely			
Amount of travel			
Benefits package			
Type or size of company			
Diversity, equity, inclusion efforts			
Corporate social responsibility (ESG)			
Quality of company leadership			
Company culture			

Christiana

I spent twenty-four years in management consulting, at the same firm the entire time, eventually making senior partner. Seeing that fact on my résumé, you might imagine that I was single-mindedly focused on the traditional path to partner, but the reality is much more interesting. I figured out fairly early on that I enjoyed working in fast-paced environments, solving tough problems, and leading teams, and determined that management consulting offered all of those conditions. I also knew that I wanted to have a family and be reliably present in my child's life. Those givens led me to carve out multiple career paths during my time with McKinsey. I was on the traditional path until my son was born, then on a part-time program (working four days a week) for ten years, then balanced conducting research with serving clients. Each of those paths helped me progress to senior partner, but the pace, intensity, and travel requirements were very different. "Flexing" within my personal guardrails enabled me to succeed in a demanding environment and enjoy the ride for a very long time.

Your Ambitions Will Evolve

In the early years of your career, one of your biggest concerns might be compensation. Key areas of focus could be earning enough money to pay back student loans, living a reasonably comfortable lifestyle, and growing a savings account. Anything positive about a job beyond that could just seem like a bonus. If that resonates, we get it! We felt the same way just out of college. Finances are often a key component to choosing a job, and sometimes putting money first might truly be the best option for you. But your goal should be moving beyond that. A career can be deeply rewarding in myriad ways, and it's essential that you be able to make choices that help you get the most value out of it.

When you're further into your career, you know more about yourself and what you're good at. As you gain new experiences, you'll find that fresh skills, passions, and talents will come to the surface. You might begin to shine in areas you hadn't even considered before. Similarly, what was once so important to you might not matter so much anymore. There's a very good chance this personal evolution will alter the original course you set out on years ago. When this happens, don't just keep driving in the same direction! Give yourself permission to change course. As mentioned, we recommend revisiting your personal guardrails once a year to assess whether everything is still a good fit. A smart time to do this is around the same time as your annual review at work. It'll help you remember to check in with yourself once a year and will serve as a reminder that you're the captain of your own ship. Review your goals from the previous year and think about how you've evolved. Are you on the right path, or should you try something new—even if it's unexpected? Don't be afraid to put the work in now for something that will pay off later.

KEY TAKEAWAYS

- Win with the career long game, not the job short game.

- Keep your eye on your Cardinal Direction.

- Ascertain your personal guardrails and update them when needed.

Grow Your Professional Equity

I like to say it's an attitude of not just thinking outside the box,
but not even seeing the box.

—Safra A. Catz, CEO of Oracle

You're probably asking yourself, "How do I keep growing? How do I stay relevant? How do I maximize my career trajectory over time?" Now that you know what Career Forward means for you, let's put some practical metrics on it.

If you're operating Career Forward, you're building equity—the same way you might do in your financial life. Only this equity gets created in your career. We call it professional equity.

As you start focusing on building professional equity, let's continue the analogy with this idea: think of yourself as a growth stock.

Simply put, a growth stock is a company that is expected to increase in value at a faster than average rate. If you think of that stock as a person, it's someone who is always looking to grow and develop and expand their career at a level significantly above average.

In the financial market, growth stocks—think of Tesla or Apple in their early years—are especially exciting because of their upward trajectory and heightened ability to create exponential shareholder value. They grow revenues and earnings at a faster rate than their competitors and have a higher profile of risk and returns than other stocks. We believe that leaders with a similar mindset are equally exciting. A growth stock mentality enables you to take ownership of your career destiny.

Growing Your Professional Value

We both know Sabrina Simmons from our time together on the Williams-Sonoma board, where for many years Sabrina chaired the committee overseeing the company's financial reporting process. Sabrina is currently a director on a number of large boards, including Columbia Sportswear, Coursera, and Petco. Prior to her board service, Sabrina was the chief financial officer (CFO) of Gap, Inc., a multibillion-dollar retailer, for over ten years.

Sabrina's career philosophy has always been: "Land yourself in a place where you can thrive, and where your values align with the company, so you feel great about working with them. Work hard and stay curious, then let the rest happen."

Sabrina made the jump to CFO when she joined a small public genetics company. She openly acknowledges that it was a learning curve. She hired a coach to help her deal with personnel issues, and the feedback was incredibly tough to hear. She learned she was coming across as a know-it-all. She learned she needed to talk less and instead invite discussion by listening a lot more to what her team had to say. Ultimately, Sabrina realized that she didn't need to be the smartest person in the room all the time.

Sabrina made a wise choice. She embraced the feedback and grew as a leader, but she also found that she was much more effective when she was passionate about the company and the product—an engaged leader is a better leader—and the genetics industry wasn't the right sector for her. That's why she was so excited to land at Gap, Inc., initially as the vice-president and treasurer. The business of fashion was something she could get excited about. However, she joined right before September 11, 2001, so she was thrown right into the deep end. As treasurer, she had to go to Wall Street and raise money for the company when a lot of potential funding entities had turned ultra-cautious. Gap needed to raise $3 billion even while the company was being downgraded by rating agencies. It was a huge challenge, and Sabrina loved it. In hindsight, it was a tremendous benefit for her career growth to have to figure things out on the fly in such urgent circumstances.

She went deep into the company, built relationships, and learned all the details of the business. She was up all night many nights, traveling on planes post-9/11, when moving through airports was crazy, but she was grateful for the chance to test her mettle and excel.

Continually throughout her career, Sabrina worked to increase her professional equity. Her message today: "Good times aren't always good for your career." You won't grow as much if business is always good. And for your team, challenges can be an incredible development opportunity.

Sabrina also follows a few invaluable guidelines. She promotes the importance of investing in relationships with your team members because it makes giving feedback easier, even when it's tough feedback. As a result of the connections she built, she was able to be very direct with her team when she needed to be. She wanted them to know that their success was her success, but that she'd be very direct ("almost brutal"). People were okay with that because they knew she was trying to do what was best for them. She was helping them build their professional equity, even as she was increasing her own.

Be a "Growth Stock"

As an employee, you're an essential part of your company's ability to create value. Your perceived worth at your organization is based on your level of consistent contribution in achieving meaningful results. As is true of an individual stock, your current performance matters, and so does your anticipated future performance.

When you think of yourself as a growth stock, it helps you get into the right frame of mind for driving professional success in the short and long term. As your stock rises, your company reaps the rewards of your performance. But just as important, you're likely to experience a host of personal benefits, such as increased compensation, a greater ability to shape your role at the company, enhanced job security, and more opportunities to transition to a desirable role at a different company.

In this mindset, you're always trying to improve yourself so that you can enhance your level of contribution. You invest in and anticipate the growth of your company, stay agile, and develop the capabilities needed for continued success. You focus on learning new things, honing your skills, and going out of your way to gain new experiences that could be valuable in your role. You take on different responsibilities, some of which may come with the risk of failure, because the chances of rewards and further growth make them worthwhile. In other words, having a growth stock mentality enables you to take ownership of your career destiny.

It's never too early to get into this frame of mind and start taking actions that build your professional equity position. This can mean attending to the smallest details.

Grace remembers a young woman at her company who consistently struggled to get her input into the conversation during team discussions. She was naturally shy, which didn't help in a group of type A peers. By failing to be heard, she missed making a meaningful contribution that could be acknowledged by others.

When Grace sat down with her over coffee, she found the young woman on the verge of despair. "Maybe I should leave the company," she said. "This isn't working." Grace didn't think that moving would solve her problem and told her so. Instead, she suggested tackling the problem head on. Grace offered a few techniques she could use to shift the dynamics of the team and open space for her to contribute. "First," she said, "assume good intent on the part of the others. They might be focused on themselves and unaware that you're struggling to participate."

Second, Grace gave her a practical strategy: "View the conversations as a bouncing ball that moves to different people across the table. Practice jumping in with a comment after the second or third person has spoken." This technique would give her a trigger point for her response. Third, if she couldn't get a word in and others were speaking over her, Grace suggested that she say, "Can we pause for a second? I have something to add."

She tried these techniques and over time was able to get more comfortable sharing, and in turn her colleagues warmed up to her and her ideas. She told Grace that she enjoyed her job more and loved making a contribution. Once this young worker was "in the game," she quickly became someone others turned to for her expertise, and in that way she began to increase her professional equity.

Those committed to building professional equity keep striving, even after they've achieved success. They never settle in and rest on their past achievements, thinking they'll be carried forward by momentum. They don't get comfortable coasting in roles where they've become familiar with what it takes to do the job, because they know this approach is bound to eventually derail. When people stop pushing themselves, their professional equity gradually declines and their compensation year over year slows in contrast to that of their peers. They're often the first to be let go when a company goes through a merger or acquisition because their contribution level isn't high enough to make them a critical asset. Ultimately, they lose control of the ability to drive their career destiny.

As an exercise, identify a job you might like to have someday, whether at your current company or another, and determine any skill set or experience gaps you have that would reduce your chances of getting hired. Ask yourself: *if I were to apply for this dream job now, what are some reasons I might not get it?* Check job descriptions and job postings whenever possible and pay attention to who gets hired for what positions, so you have a solid idea of what ideal candidates look like for various roles.

Thinking of yourself as a growth stock is not only a smart move for you as an individual, but also the best thing you can do for your employer. This mentality goes beyond general loyalty and focuses on what companies truly want: performance. When you have a learning mindset and an insatiable appetite for driving results and growing professionally, you and the organization will thrive.

Christiana

Like a lot of people who start out in management consulting, I never expected to stay as long as I did. I loved the work, though, which is why I stayed with McKinsey & Company for so many years. Even as I focused on progressing from associate to senior partner, I remained very conscious of how I could best prepare myself for success outside of consulting. I built expertise in a specific industry (retail, particularly e-commerce), sought out proprietary research opportunities at the company, wrote articles, spoke at industry conferences to raise my profile, and cultivated a widening network of professional relationships. Although I didn't have any set plans to leave the firm, I wanted to create demand for myself in the market in case my situation at McKinsey changed for whatever reason. As an example, whenever a recruiter reached out to me about a potential role, I took the call, even when I wasn't looking to make a change. That way I learned about new professional opportunities and kept tabs on who was hiring, as well as what kinds of skills were in demand in the retail industry. While I was committed to the firm, I couldn't forget the reality that I was a single mom and the sole breadwinner for my family. I thought about this approach as a way of creating a portfolio of options for myself, knowing that one or more of those options might pay off in the future.

Over more than two decades at McKinsey, I often received job offers from other companies—typically my close clients. I considered making a move, but it wasn't worth it to leave when I had more and more reasons to stay, whether through promotions, compensation increases, or flexible work arrangements. Eventually, after ten years as a senior partner, I felt that my opportunities for growth were finally greater outside McKinsey. Because I'd built a sizable network of industry contacts and client executives, I just put the word out across a small number of companies about my desire to find an external leadership role. When I left the firm for a senior role at Nike, even though I'd been at the same company for most of my professional life, the transition was much easier than it would have been if

I hadn't viewed myself as a growth stock. I felt prepared to learn new skills, totally shake things up, and be a little uncomfortable for a while, since that's the way I'd already been approaching my career up to that point.

Look for Your Equity-Building Opportunities

Bold moves can provide an accelerated path to building professional equity. Taking on new challenges, especially in changing business environments, naturally enables growth. The one wrinkle? These often require a leap of faith that you will succeed regardless of the risk in circumstances.

At one point in Grace's career, when she was a single mom and the primary financial provider for her family, she decided to leave a very comfortable position at Kraft Foods, where she led a team in the purchasing, packaging, and indirect materials, for a new position that seemed like a huge risk. The job as chief procurement officer for United Airlines involved oversight of more than $13 billion annually in corporate purchasing, covering categories like jet fuel, corporate real estate leases, landing fees, IT, HR benefits, airline maintenance components, onboard services, and airport operation services. She also had to establish a new operating model, which involved developing new capabilities and finding new resources.

The move placed her in an industry with a history of bankruptcy, operational challenges, and labor/management tensions. Her friends couldn't understand why she would leave a stable, reputable company for a new role that was plagued with risk.

Grace wasn't swayed by their fears. For her, it was simple: The toughest jobs and business environments can yield the best growth and opportunities to contribute. She'd always been attracted to transformational opportunities, and this was certainly one of those.

Grace also knew that airlines had very lean and flat executive management structures, so this job would be different from those she'd had within other large corporate structures. It would give her a chance to engage with the strategic decisions of the company beyond her functional role. Having a growth stock mentality, she considered this a huge draw.

United's CEO was leading a major business transformation. In addition to addressing the challenges involved in turning around the airline, Grace gained the opportunity to reshape the company's global procurement function. This was a significant transformation in itself, from accelerating the adoption of improved sourcing practices to bringing in fresh talent from other industries.

Grace loved the job, and within a year she could see that the airline's initiatives were finding momentum. But just at that moment the global financial crisis hit. Airlines were gravely impacted. "I worry that our stock is dropping toward the price of a grande latte," Grace once said to her boss. She wasn't kidding. It was a grave situation.

However, on reflection, Grace could see that working through a challenging transformation and an economic crisis at the airline gave her invaluable experience and skills in leading during adversity, solving complex problems, and helping employees weather uncertainty. In the end, her team contributed to improved profitability in several categories, as well as higher performance and a financially beneficial merger with another airline. She also walked away with a sense of pride in having become a better leader from this experience. Taking the job was a risky career move, but it paid off. Not only was she able to help the company improve shareholder value, but she also gained a wealth of experience that boosted her personal stock, which served her well as she landed her next big job.

Equity's Other Meaning

It's interesting that the word *equity* has two meanings. One refers to value, which is the primary way we're using it here. But the other definition of equity means equality, so tuck that idea in the back of your mind. An equal status for women increases their equity (value).

Enabling women to achieve greater equity in the workplace is not just a worthy personal goal. It makes sense for companies because more diverse leadership teams help them perform better. We've seen this firsthand across many organizations, and numerous studies have proven the advantages:

- Diverse management boosts revenue by 19 percent.[1]
- Executive teams that are highly gender diverse are found to be 21 percent more likely to outperform on profitability.[2]
- Companies in the top quartile for gender diversity are 15 percent more likely to have financial returns above their respective national industry medians.[3]
- Compared with individuals, diverse teams make better decisions 87 percent of the time.[4]
- Companies with above-average total diversity earn 19 percent higher innovation revenues on average.[5]
- When companies foster an inclusive work culture, 83 percent of millennials are found to be more actively engaged, versus 60 percent in less inclusive environments.[6]

Now that so many executive teams are aware of the extent to which gender diversity in leadership impacts their bottom line, they're more motivated to promote top female talent. In fact, we're seeing exponential changes in how companies support their female employees. That's a good trend.

Take Note of the Equity Players

In every organization there are individuals who get pulled into the most exciting strategic initiatives. Everyone seems to want their opinion, and everything they touch seems to turn to gold. Who are these people at your organization? How have they earned so much equity? By studying these "equity players," you can uncover the elements that drive their success. And by building relationships with them, you may build your own equity.

Keep in mind that these people aren't necessarily the most senior on staff. You don't need to cozy up to the CEO, which is an overreach for most people. Equity players exist at every level, some of which may be at levels under you and in a variety of functional areas. But if you know what to look for, you'll spot equity players who create the organizational current that can drive change and accelerate the personal equity of others. In our own careers, we found that having strong relationships with the top performers in our organization paid off in discreet and overt ways. We recommend you do the same, creating a strategy around identifying those people and finding ways to win introductions and meaningful interactions with them. Building your connections in this strategic way will pay dividends over time as your professional network expands and becomes even more valuable.

HOW TO SPOT THE EQUITY PLAYERS

Equity players:

- are promoted/selected for representation and messaging at company forums and meetings.
- are often chosen to lead highly visible strategic company projects.
- appear to get CEO, C-suite, and board exposure.

- are sought out behind the scenes by employees and peers for personal and professional opinions.
- tend to advance quickly in role or scope.
- have input that carries weight and drives decisions or actions.
- are happy, energized, and confident.

Are You Building Equity?

How do you know you're building your professional equity—within your organization and over your career? This chart provides some helpful checkpoints.

CAREER EQUITY CHECKPOINTS

INFLUENCE	COMPENSATION
You are often under consideration for big events.	You are well compensated and can negotiate your terms.
Your company makes accommodations for you.	Your company is proactive about salary progression, and your compensation is continuing to grow at a rapid pace.
Your opinion is decisive in discussions about which direction to take.	
GROWTH OPPORTUNITIES	**RESPECT**
You're considered the one to watch.	Others ask, "What do you think?" when they're faced with important decisions. You're considered a beacon, the one to go to.
You have an influential individual as a mentor.	
You regularly have access to learning and growth opportunities.	You have a reputation for being effective, fair, and a leader.

For true professional equity, you'll want to check at least three and ideally all four of these boxes over time. People sometimes make the mistake of thinking that because they're being well compensated or they're receiving interesting assignments, their career is moving in the right direction. But that's not always the case.

Watch Out for Benevolent Stagnation

A young colleague of Grace's once asked her for advice about making her next move. (We'll call her Sharon to protect her identity.) Sharon was interested in progressing in their organization. Grace knew her as a high-capacity performer—smart, engaged, and effective. She was the person in the organization people relied on when they needed someone to lead a complex project.

Despite her obvious abilities and contributions, Sharon had never advanced beyond a certain level. She was well paid and had job security, but she was not progressing in her career.

When Grace began to talk to Sharon about her lack of growth prospects, she recognized that Sharon was one of those indispensable performers the organization appreciated and relied on to get complex work done, but that it wasn't invested in her professional growth. Her superiors *wanted* her to stay put. Sharon was actually happy with the situation—until one day she woke up and realized she wanted something more.

There's a benevolent form of stagnation that companies often impose on well-performing employees. The salary may be good. The work may be important. But such employees are not going anywhere. If you're on a growth stock path, you're less likely to let this situation happen to you.

There's an oft-mentioned management principle called the Peter principle, developed by Laurence J. Peter. According to the principle, the typical hierarchical management structure allows for people to be continually promoted based on past achievements—with skills that are not necessarily transferable—until they reach a point where they are incompetent. They will then fail to earn further promotions, plateauing at a point above their competency.

Most of us have known embodiments of the Peter principle. The concept of building career equity is the opposite. If you adopt this growth stock mindset combined with the Career Forward principle, you can anticipate and build the skills needed to remain competent—even with an enlarged role. We want to emphasize that although career plateaus can happen at some point in your career, you *can* overcome them by staying focused on growth.

The growth stock mantra is simple: Be excellent at what you do, look for chances to grow your network and your capabilities, and stay aware of external opportunities. Even if your company is hitting its numbers and everything is going swimmingly, don't relax and get too comfortable. There is always more you could be doing to better set yourself up for success later. That's why you should commit to always performing at your highest level of ability.

When you're pushing yourself to be the best, you're playing both the long game and short game, knowing there will be ups and downs along the way. You can expect years of exceptionally hard work, resiliency, and constant learning, but it will be worth it. There's something exhilarating about seeing how far you can go. Undoubtably you'll learn and evolve in unexpected ways throughout your life and the stages of your career. But if you're always focusing on improving your ability to contribute, you'll be incredibly well positioned for whatever direction life takes you. Growth stock leaders steer their own boats and career destiny.

EXERCISE: THE SOAR METHOD

Your boss will let you know when you're excelling on the job, but how will you know when your *career* isn't progressing? Try this assessment tool, which we've developed to help people determine how their professional progress aligns (or doesn't) with their career goals. Our SOAR template stands for strengths, opportunities, actions, and red flags. We recommend doing this exercise once a year, to check in with yourself and your progress against your goals, using a simple four-box matrix:

Strengths: What skills and capabilities are you becoming known for? What strengths do you want to focus on developing next?

Opportunities: What professional opportunities are you excited about pursuing—for example, new work areas, a global scope, broader responsibilities, continuing education, etc.?

Actions: What specific steps do you need to take in the next year to capture the opportunities identified above?

Red Flags: What pitfalls or potential derailers are on the horizon? What technical gaps may you have in comparison with competitors for those opportunities? What contingencies can you create to help avoid them?

Annual SOAR Assessment

Let's make SOAR real. Here's an example that reflects Christiana's personal assessment when she was a manager at McKinsey, looking to move up to more senior roles. Use this example as a guide to fill in your own boxes.

CHRISTIANA'S SOAR, AS A MID-LEVEL MANAGER	
STRENGTHS • Able to solve tough, ambiguous problems. • Inspirational team leader.	**OPPORTUNITIES** • Stepping up to the next level of client leadership. • Clientele development.
ACTIONS • Get feedback from senior partners on my development plan. • Create client priority target list and pursue with colleagues.	**RED FLAGS** • Not getting strongest associates put on my teams. • Not being asked to sit in on a partner meeting.

Remember that growth stocks are future focused. That automatically puts you in a dynamic process, as norms, expectations, and what is valued will change over time. Make it a practice to pay attention to how the business environment is changing so that you are aware of unmet or evolving demands. If you know which way things are moving, you can be strategic about building new skills that will become an asset to you and your company. Also pay attention to your own skills and learning curve, making sure they align with your growth plan.

When you learn to think more like a growth stock, you'll begin to keep a better eye on the return on investment (ROI) you're getting as a result of your work. You'll see how a certain skill, connection, or bit of knowledge opened a door and boosted you to a higher level. This will help you continue to properly evaluate new possibilities and decide where to best focus your efforts.

KEY TAKEAWAYS

- Think like a growth stock.

- Surround yourself with high performers.

- Know how to assess and grow your professional equity.

- Recognize the signs of potential stagnation . . .
  and early success.

4

Get Full Value

The extent to which you're bringing true, sustainable value to the organization, compared with others, is your internal equity, and should in part drive your paycheck.

**— Robin L. Pinkley, PhD,
creator of the Gain-Gain Approach to Profitable Negotiation**

"Give the number first." That's the negotiating gem Bozoma Saint John, former Netflix chief marketing officer, offered in a CBS interview about salary negotiations. She added, "Make it as high as hell, because then you can't be lowballed. Do the work. Don't just call a number out of the sky. Know the range and then exceed the range because then you can negotiate down just a little bit."[1] St. John's bold advice is welcome because salary negotiation is often a confusing and intimidating process.

Are you getting paid what you're worth? As we've said, compensation is only one piece of your value assessment. However, no one would dispute that it's critical, along with being an area where women face persistent difficulties. If you're not commanding fair compensation you can't grow.

In an ideal world, we would all be offered salary and benefits packages that directly reflect our performance. Unfortunately, that isn't reality. Even when hiring managers do their best to pay people fairly, compensation is affected by multiple factors, including how well you negotiate for what you're worth.

We know that there's a gender pay gap. According to a Pew Research Center analysis of median hourly earnings of both full- and part-time workers, in 2022, women earned 82 percent of what men earned.[2] This gap is closing due to good efforts by companies, but work remains. It's difficult to change people's unconscious biases about men's and women's ability to do the same job, but it's within our power to educate ourselves about what we're worth and to make sure our employers are aware of the facts.[3]

The compensation narrative isn't just about fairness. As much as we care about advancing women in the workplace because it's the right thing to do, we know that where compensation equity exists, it makes a huge difference in how people feel about their jobs, as well as the lifestyles they're able to afford. The gender pay gap is substantial when you consider a single year's wages, but it's colossal over an entire career.

Over the course of her lifetime, the average woman worker loses more than $530,000 because of the gender wage gap, and the average college-educated woman loses even more—nearly $800,000.[4] And those figures don't even take into account how much this chunk of money could grow if you invested it over time, which is a key strategy for creating wealth.

The bottom line is, once a woman falls behind, she may never close the gap. That's why you've got to get paid what you're worth early on, not just later. You can't make up the difference if you don't start at the right place.

The first thing to know about compensation is that it's almost always negotiable. This is true whether you're contending for a newly created role or a recently vacated position, or you're staying in the same job at your company. It might feel uncomfortable to ask for a raise or make a counteroffer, but it's an essential part of achieving fair compensation.

One of our friends told us that all her male direct reports would ask for raises at their annual reviews, but this was the case for only one of her female direct reports. Our friend realized that the women who reported to her did not know that it was acceptable— and common—for employees to ask for a compensation increase at these regular checkpoints. Part of the reason the gender wage gap exists is that men tend to ask for increases more frequently than women do. Companies don't set out to pay men more, but they do respond to negotiations. Christiana can relate to this, since she never negotiated her comp until after she left consulting and took a senior role in a public company.

When it comes to compensation, you have a lot to think about and a variety of nuances to consider. But the biggest takeaway is that you need to advocate for yourself. Don't be afraid to speak up to get what you need. Between the two of us, we have a combined several decades in workplaces where we climbed the ladder within organizations, changed companies and industries, and were on the managing and hiring end for numerous employees. The following is our best advice for knowing—and getting—what you're worth.

1. Do your research.

In an effort to achieve gender parity, many public companies are now required by law to disclose their gender pay gap. So if ever there was a moment to educate yourself on compensation, it's now. Do your research online to see what you can find out. Talk to recruiters and peers at other companies to gain insight on what similar roles are paying. Make sure you fully understand how the stock grant package works if that's part of your compensation. This will ground your opinion and give you reference data. We recommend doing this work every few years, as well as every time you change companies. Remember that small changes in compensation add up over time, and the compounding effect of investing your money can be significant, so don't put this off.

Learn where you can go to find advice about fair compensation and engage with others willing to share their compensation information. For example, Glassdoor (glassdoor.com) is a great online resource, as is Levels.fyi. Both use millions of salaries to determine what the market is currently paying for your job where you live, offers sound advice about negotiating, and hosts a community of sharing. You can also check out professional associations in your field. Best of all, talk to peers. As the saying goes, knowledge is power.

Increasingly, there are laws in place to promote compensation transparency. Even so, those in your workplace may foster an implicit understanding that nobody talks about salaries. This silence can be tenacious, but openness can be risky, too. Even if it's perfectly legal to share compensation information, you might risk your boss's disapproval. We've also seen situations in which employees pool their compensation data and ratchet up tension in a company. Deciding whether to share comp data is a decision individuals need to make for themselves, but we believe it's only a matter of time before most companies take a more open posture. For one simple reason—their employees are demanding it.

As you get into more senior roles, it may make sense to hire a compensation consultant or pay an external service for salary data when you're considering a job offer. Many people don't know these types of services exist for individuals, but they can be invaluable when interviewing for a new role, their onetime cost more than justified by what would otherwise be forfeited in compounded earnings over time.

Christiana

When I moved from McKinsey to Nike, it was the first time that I needed to understand corporate compensation. McKinsey's partnership structure was completely different. My first instinct when Nike made the offer was to say, "I'll take it." I thought it was a good offer. But a colleague persuaded me to get an outside compensation service to help advise me. I hired a fairly junior person at a reasonable cost, and he reviewed the offer. He demystified things I didn't understand. He highlighted things that I would've let slide, like fewer paid-time-off days and a narrower relocation package. In the end, I negotiated the improvements in my package myself, but with more information and insight. When there was one last issue, not a big deal, I decided to go back a second time and they met me halfway. I felt good about the process and appreciated how much I'd learned—not to mention the sheer confidence I'd built. Even though I'd been in a senior role for a long time, this was a new arena, and I took advantage of the opportunity to equip myself with knowledge before I dove in.

2. Read the tea leaves.

When you learn you're being undercompensated, you still need to be strategic about the right time to initiate a conversation about an increase. If the business environment isn't great and the company is underperforming, you probably want to hold off asking for more money. Even if higher-ups know you deserve it, lousy timing can signal that you're not focused on what's best for the company—and such poor judgment could affect your professional equity. On the flip side, if you hold off asking for a raise until business is absolutely booming, you'll be waiting longer than necessary. Pay attention to what's happening in the company and think ahead so you can optimize your timing.

3. Recognize a change in job scope.

Roles have a way of flexing and morphing over time. As a growth stock, you want to add value, lead special projects, and fill critical gaps. However, top performers may find that the day-to-day scope of their role is much different from what was promised on paper in the job description. From added responsibilities to dealing with a much higher level of complexity, many people experience scope creep in their jobs. When this happens, you need to consider whether your role is now worth higher compensation. Years ago, Grace found herself in this position when she realized that over time the scope of her job had expanded significantly to a point well beyond the pay level at which she was originally hired. She summarized the expanded job responsibilities, approached her superiors for consideration, and led with the facts. The company agreed with the data she presented, and they gave her a considerable raise in base pay and bonuses.

4. Negotiate.

You may worry that asking for more money can irritate bosses and hiring managers and cause lasting damage to relationships.

On the contrary, we've seen how negotiating compensation can actually set a more positive tone for employees—especially new hires. Coming back with a counter-request demonstrates that you're confident, know your worth, and have awareness that other companies would want to pay you fairly. In some ways, it balances the power dynamic and shows that you expect to be treated with respect. That's not to say there won't be individual managers who respond poorly, but, overall, being confident is a win.

You may be uncertain about how to negotiate or unsure about what the best practices are in effective negotiations. It's not a skill that is explicitly taught or even talked about at most companies. We recommend you take a negotiations course at some point early in your career if you want to learn the basics and get a chance to practice with experts. Many business schools and professional associations offer negotiation training online, so you should be able to find something helpful relatively easily and at a very reasonable cost.

Some basic tactics that you may want to use:

- Get the highest base salary that you can get in your initial offer, since all future raises will be a percentage of that.
- Start with your ceiling, not your floor—remember Bozoma Saint John's advice at the beginning of this chapter. Back up your ask with tangible examples that show why you deserve the compensation.
- Ask yourself what matters most to you when you think about comp: cash, equity, flexibility (that is to say, time off, less travel, a day off to be with your kid, etc.). Use those as your bargaining chips.
- Try to avoid taking the first offer even if you're happy with it or it's your first job.

Getting your best compensation is a matter of what's negotiable and what's not, and what's worth it and what's not. Be aware of how you show up in the negotiation. Keep a positive tone. This should be a win-win, where you're paid what you're worth and your employer retains a valuable team member. If there are things you want to ask for that will make a lot of noise, you need to decide if they're worth going to the mat.

Grace

I saw from an early age how vital money is when it comes to taking care of yourself and others, so compensation was a big focus for me as I progressed up the ladder. When my parents immigrated to the United States from Cuba, they had very little money and few belongings. They had to figure out how to make a life for themselves with very limited means. To me, financial security and a strong work ethic was a path to taking care of family.

I started babysitting at age eleven, and from then on, I always had a job. I worked part time throughout high school at a bakery, which required early morning starting times on the weekends. In college, I worked part time in the cafeteria to pay for my education while carrying a full load of classes. I appreciated having the opportunity to work and found satisfaction in being able to earn my own money. I saw that money was empowering, as it bought freedom and options. So instead of piddling my earnings away at the mall, I saved and saved as much as I could.

Later in life after I started my own family, my priority of earning good money and saving it proved to be crucial.

My husband and I divorced when my kids were four and seven. I focused on building a financial safety net early by living below my means and saving. That ultimately gave me the option to make certain career decisions on the basis of factors beyond compensation. And some of those bold moves paid off handsomely later in accelerated career growth.

5. Don't overdo it.

Negotiating is tricky—it's something you always want to do, but there's an invisible line you shouldn't cross. Be strategic. When you are considering a new offer, a typical approach is to counteroffer twice, which often works well. These two rounds are especially important if you need to relocate and uproot your life for a new role. It's smart to circle back to hiring managers to confirm important details on everything from pay to bonuses to vacation days and relocation funds. But know when to declare victory. Continuing to push for more and more will not serve you well in the end if it taints the organization's view of you before you even start. Equally self-sabotaging is accepting an offer and then coming back to negotiate after the fact.

6. Pay it forward.

Once you've achieved a certain level of professional success, make a difference by assuring that your rising tide lifts other boats. No woman's success exists in a vacuum. We achieve in a collective effort to create a world where equality is an automatic reality. Each of us had support when we were coming up, and paying it forward was a big motivation for writing this book. So as you reach a level where you have influence, here are a few ways you can make a difference for the women coming behind you:

As a baseline, don't tolerate sexism in your team or division. Call it out when you see it. At the same time, be on the lookout for unconscious bias.

Make a point of offering feedback and encouragement to women, even in small ways, whenever the opportunity presents itself, and look for chances to recommend and mentor women. Be an advocate for the talented women who work for you.

As you reach more senior levels, you'll have opportunities to be supportive of compensation equity in your organization. We've both sat on compensation committees and found them excellent places to help level the playing field for women. Compensation calculations can feel like cold mathematical equations where everyone is judged by the same metrics, but if you look deeper, you can find some of those hidden biases at work that penalize diverse employees in ways that are unfair. The first thing to do is make sure the compensation reviews include the diversity and inclusion lens, looking at gender and people of color, and other dimensions of difference. In the past, before companies started assessing their compensation practices from these angles, white males automatically received higher ratings than women and people of color. It *matters*.

. . . . .

Finally, to realize your worth to your employer, stay laser focused on how you can achieve the best version of your capabilities. Set your own path and remain open to resetting the bar every day. That's how you show up for your company and add as much value as possible in your role.

KEY TAKEAWAYS

- Do your research—there's lots available now.

- Know your worth in dollars and influence.

- Keep the tone positive. Get to a win-win.

- Be a smart negotiator. Study best practices.

5

The Underdog's Superpower

I personally love being underestimated. I think it's a total superpower.

—Bumble CEO Whitney Wolfe Herd at the Aspen Ideas Festival in Aspen, 2022

Shalini Sharp, an accomplished leader in the pharmaceutical industry, rose to top executive levels at an early age. She spent fifteen years as CFO at two companies, Agenus and Ultragenya and is currently a board member and advisor to multiple publicly traded life sciences companies and nonprofit organizations.

Shalini's parents emigrated from India before she was born, and she was always aware of being a bit of an outsider. While her parents were extremely encouraging, sometimes there could be sexism inherent in Indian culture back then. When she was accepted at Harvard, for example, there was a suggestion that she do the laundry and cooking for her male cousins in Boston.

Shalini rose above those cultural stereotypes, but when she became a CFO at age thirty-one, she wasn't sure if it was age, gender, or culture that made her feel that she had something to prove. Were people wondering, *Does she actually know what she's doing? Do I have to listen to her?*

How did she address it? "I worked hard to make sure that I was never caught flat-footed, and I showed people that I could be an ally and help them with their goals," she told us. "I tried to create goodwill." As a result, she had people say to her, "Now I know the next time you ask me for something, I'll do it, because it's going to be worthwhile." She observed, "Sometimes you end up with allies this way, and they might even feel a loyalty to you as a result."

Not only did Shalini rise above being an underdog, but she built strategic relationships by showing she could be a trusted ally. She added, "I also think being an underdog can actually be motivating by giving you something to prove."

Everyone has been an underdog at some time in their careers. We've all been novices, not quite up to speed. Many of us have entered new fields or unfamiliar work cultures. And even more experienced women can find themselves feeling like underdogs in new situations.

It's not uncommon for women to be underestimated, sometimes without even knowing it. The key is to acknowledge the challenges of being in an underdog position, but not to let it break your spirit. The surprising news is that being an underdog can be a powerful benefit, creating unexpected opportunities to break out. So what does it really mean to be an underdog, what drives it, and how can women flip the dynamic and use it to their advantage?

Why Women Can Fall Behind

According to the 2022 report "Women in the Workplace" by LeanIn and McKinsey & Company—now in its eighth year—women are still facing barriers large and small to achieving the positions and respect they've earned and deserve. For example:

- Among employees who switched jobs in the past two years, 48 percent of women leaders say they did so because they wanted more opportunity to advance.

- Thirty-seven percent of women leaders have had a coworker get credit for their idea, compared to 27 percent of men leaders.
- Women leaders are twice as likely as men leaders to be mistaken for someone more junior.[1]

These might seem like incidental setbacks, but they reveal the deep-seated frustration women experience when they strive to get noticed and advance. According to the report's summary, "Women leaders are just as ambitious as men, but at many companies, they face headwinds that signal it will be harder to advance. They're more likely to experience belittling microaggressions, such as having their judgment questioned or being mistaken for someone more junior. They're doing more to support employee well-being and foster inclusion, but this critical work is spreading them thin and going mostly unrewarded. If companies don't act, they risk losing not only their current women leaders but also the next generation of women leaders."[2]

Sometimes the issue is unconscious bias. Everyone holds unconscious beliefs about various social and identity groups. These stereotypes cause us to quickly categorize people, even when we're not aware of doing so. Women are often the target of these stereotypes in a work environment, which may place them at a disadvantage. Our friend Pamela Neferkará, former vice president of marketing at Nike, who built a successful career as a brand leader in the sports industry, tells the story of interviewing for a particular role when one of the interviewers told her she was so impressive that he couldn't believe she wasn't already in a similar position. "The implication was, there must be something wrong with you," Pamela said. "And there was nothing wrong with me. There had been something really wrong with the system. And I think that's so important for people to continue to keep in mind."

As an African American, Pamela was always conscious that she was going to stand out. Often, she was the only person of color in the room, and sometimes the only woman. Her parents had always coached her when she was young: "You don't have the luxury of showing up unprepared." Pamela took the advice to heart, and it helped her excel early in her career when she was a junior marketing person.

"I would say from the beginning of my career, I quickly became known as someone who was always very buttoned up, very organized, very on top of details. And I kind of became the go-to whenever there was a question about 'Hey, what was decided in that meeting?' Or 'What did so-and-so say?' Or 'Do you have a copy of the report?' Because back then there was a lot of paper." Her thinking was simple: "If I was going to have all eyes on me, then how could I use that to my advantage by providing value?"

Grace

Every level I've climbed to on the career ladder, I've had fewer and fewer women peers. This has been true across all the companies I've worked for over the years. Until recently, there just haven't been a lot of women in top-level leadership roles.

People have been analyzing this gender diversity issue for years. I've come across plenty of books and articles framed around the idea that for a woman to make it in a "man's world," she must just accept unconscious bias. I'm glad we're reaching a point in time where saying that kind of thing is no longer considered acceptable.

To be successful at anything, you must be authentic. That's where your power comes from. I always counsel women to be authentic and develop a nuanced approach to unapologetically going after what they want.

Although women have made tremendous progress in the workforce in past decades, the success prototype for a leader is still often seen as male rather than female. According to the Clayman Institute for Gender Research at Stanford, "Research consistently finds that women have less influence in group settings, their contributions are judged less positively, and they are less likely to get credit for their ideas."[3] That's because the prototype—the one we're used to seeing in leadership positions—is male. This is also true in other professional arenas, such as politics, medicine, religion, and education.

The bias is so pervasive that knee-jerk assumptions get made about women's potential before there's even time to make an objective evaluation.

Christiana

I applied to Harvard Business School because it was the top school. On the day when most of the people I worked with got their acceptance letters, I didn't receive one. My boyfriend at the time was a couple years older than me and had already graduated from Harvard Business School. That night he brought dinner over, and I guess to make me feel better, he laid out all the rejection letters he'd ever received. I was flabbergasted. "I didn't get turned down yet," I reminded him. "I just haven't received my letter." The next day my acceptance letter came. I broke up with my boyfriend shortly afterward because I didn't want to be with someone who didn't believe in my potential. His first assumption was that I'd failed.

As we've repeatedly pointed out, as a woman in business, you'll often find yourself underestimated or overlooked due to unconscious bias.

For example, studies have shown that men are more likely to get the benefit of the doubt when it comes to promotions. Managers may unconsciously believe men can stretch into new roles and be successful, while women are often expected to prove themselves first, and even then can get passed over for promotions they deserve.

A recent study conducted by researchers at Yale and MIT analyzed a retail chain with 30,000 employees, where 56 percent of entry-level staff are women. You might expect that this ratio would remain the same at all levels of the company, but that wasn't the case. The study found that even though women tended to score slightly higher than their male counterparts on annual performance assessments, they were 14 percent less likely to be promoted at the company each year. When researchers analyzed the performance rubrics, they found that on average, managers rated the growth potential for female employees lower than that of male employees, regardless of whether their past performance was high.

"It appears that they were held to a higher standard," says Yale professor Kelly Shue, who led the study. Women were simply not given the benefit of the doubt at the same level as men, especially when it came to promotions.[4]

When the Bar Gets (Unfairly) Raised

Another dynamic that can make women feel like underdogs at work is the constantly raised bar. A woman will perform at a high level and leaders will be impressed, but then they'll raise the bar higher, wanting her to demonstrate success repeatedly before they feel confident in promoting her. Grace has described this dynamic as "lapping," where female leaders with high levels of performance are expected to repeat the performance before credit leading to advancement is realized. This can burn valuable time. Frustratingly, when a man performs well, leaders are typically more confident that he can do it again and refrain from asking him to complete another "lap."

Countless times we've observed circumstances where women are told, "It's great that you can do X, but how about Y and Z?" It reminds us of the famous story about iconic dancers Fred Astaire and Ginger Rogers. Astaire received most of the acclaim, but as former Texas governor Ann Richards once observed, "Ginger Rogers did everything he did; she just did it backwards and in high heels."

LeanIn.org has studied the issue of what it calls performance bias. In a video on the topic, it was noted: "Performance bias is based on deep-rooted—and incorrect—assumptions about women's and men's abilities. We tend to underestimate women's performance, and overestimate men's." In fact, the research points out, "Women are often hired based on past accomplishments, and men are often hired based on future potential."[5] It's just another way of expecting proof before making a commitment.

It can be frustrating when higher-ups keep looking for more proof points, but the ability to rise to the occasion can become a superpower. Former secretary of state Condoleezza Rice is familiar with this reality. She grew up in segregated Birmingham, and her parents taught her that she had to be "twice as good as everyone else." It's a lesson, she says, that applies not only in that challenging environment but to all of us.[6]

You don't want to dwell on being an underdog, but you do need to recognize when people are underestimating you so you can do a strategic and intentional course correction.

Shalini Sharp has a useful perspective about how to build an inner confidence that helps you stand out in a positive way. "When men are offered a job, the stereotype is that they take it and run with it," she said. "A woman with the same qualifications might hedge and say, 'I'm not sure I can do that.' I think you need to have a little bit of brashness and a willingness to trust in yourself that you will make it."

Debunking Old Tropes

As you accelerate into your career, you're probably going to find yourself in situations where you're at the limit of your current expertise and experience. Christiana remembers a younger Nike team member, Jodi, who was asked to go to China to run Nike's outlet store business, even though she'd never lived or worked outside the United States before. Jodi confided in Christiana that she felt like she'd just been "thrown into the deep end of the pool without a floatie." Christiana told her this was a good problem to have, because it was a sign of Jodi's success, but acknowledged that it could still feel pretty daunting in the moment.

Two concepts come up in traditional career advice about these moments: "Fake it 'til you make it" and "impostor syndrome." These aren't new concepts— both have origins in the 1970s—and they're often used interchangeably to describe how you might feel and react to being in "deep water" professional situations. We'd like to give you a different way of looking at them so they empower you instead of discouraging you.

We look at "fake it 'til you make it" as a useful Jedi mind trick in which you express confidence even when you don't feel it. It's most effective as an underlying encouragement, especially when you're trying something for the first time. Expertise can take a while to build, even after you start performing an assignment, but self-confidence is a habit you can develop with focus and practice. For instance, one of our friends used to hype herself up every morning in the mirror when she was stepping up to a more senior role at work. She'd assume the "power pose" (feet apart, hands on hips) and tell herself that she was a great boss. Whatever affirmation works for you, our advice is to keep telling yourself, "I've got this," while you figure out how you're going to deliver the necessary results. In other words, retrain yourself to focus more on how you're going to make this new situation work and less on how much you may have to *fake* it while you learn.

Where "fake it 'til you make it" *doesn't* work is when you're lying about your capabilities or pretending to know something you don't know. It's okay to not know everything when you're just starting out, but you need to have a specific plan for how you're going to master the necessary learning as quickly as possible. This was the case for Christiana early in her career, when she had to get comfortable speaking in public. Overcoming a lisp as well as presentation anxiety onstage took time, practice, and a lot of coaching, but the way she achieved it was to stand up, *do* it, then do it better every time.

There will be times where you're going to have to buckle up and do something that's a little scary and a little hard. Our advice is to embrace the challenge and the uncertainty. Think of it this way: you're embracing where you're at and what you have. You're owning it. You're assuming the role. You're not faking it, you're stepping up to it.

Impostor syndrome is different. It describes an anxiety about success caused by a deep-seated sense that a promotion or other career advancement isn't earned or deserved. We've read lots of articles about professional women in particular feeling like impostors when they get to higher levels of success, but this syndrome could apply to anyone who is nagged by the feeling of being a fraud.

We reject this mindset outright, considering it the polar opposite of Career Forward. If you're thinking, *I'm not sure I belong here . . . I'm not sure I earned this . . . I'm not sure I'm capable,* you're selling yourself short. If you land a challenging job or get promoted, pat yourself on the back. It didn't happen by accident. It happened because you've shown that you can do the work, and people have confidence in you. If faking it 'til you make it is a positive mind trick for moving forward in challenging career situations, the impostor syndrome is a mind trap, one that can cause you to tread water instead of learning to swim.

If you believe that you belong where you are, if you believe that you've earned the role that you're playing, stand up for yourself. You might be an underdog for any number of reasons, including being new to a job, but approaching your work with confidence is the best way to move out of the underdog zone. Keep in mind that nobody knows everything when they start in a new position or job.

Find ways to turn self-doubt into empowerment. When you're feeling uncertain, remember the successes you've had in the past and consider what led to them. Maybe it was working harder or being bold when the moment called for it. Women can easily become their own greatest critics, so instead be your own biggest fan.

Once in the job, let the learning curve empower you. If you find your job requires deeper expertise, set out to acquire it. Ask for help. Do your homework. One advantage of being an underdog is that people will be more open to helping you—you're not a threat. Take advantage of that, like Jodi did when she accepted the promotion and transfer to China. She reached out to colleagues who'd made similar moves and asked them for coaching and advice. She researched the local market and business customs. She studied the financials of the business she was going to lead and prepared thoughts on growth opportunities. And when she finally landed in Shanghai, she arranged a "new-leader off-site" with her new team so they could spend time together and begin to bond. Formulating a concrete plan and taking these steps helped Jodi move quickly from faking it to making it as a successful leader in her new role.

CONFIDENCE CHECKLIST

- Build relationships, become empathetic. Being human is always a winning strategy.

- Be direct with your boss. Don't wallow in frustration. Be open about your aspirations and abilities. If you are being underestimated at work, think about what your bosses are getting wrong—where are their perceptions inaccurate?

- Find ways to continue to learn. Depending on your profession, there are usually opportunities to take classes or seminars online.

- Volunteer. If you raise your hand in response to a request, it will get you noticed as a team player. Just don't make it a regular, predictable behavior. (That will make you an underdog.)

- Find a mentor. The best way to find a mentor is to network. Be open to meeting colleagues, attend professional associations, and ask your network for advice.

- Advocate for yourself. Don't leave it to others.

- Be brave. It seems counterintuitive, but being an underdog can be a comfortable corner to rest in. It takes courage to step outside your comfort zone and get noticed.

- Pay it forward. Help and inspire others to succeed. It will come back to you a hundredfold.

The Underdog's Superpowers

If you think we're painting a discouraging picture of what women face when they try to advance in the workplace, we have good news. Although no one would choose to be an underdog, there is a silver lining. In fact, there are four. We've found that being an underdog can create the opportunity to develop four strengths that are so valuable we call them superpowers. They are support, confidence, motivation, and resilience.

Superpower: Support

When a woman crushes it at her job, there can be more of a wow factor than when a man succeeds—especially in male-dominated industries. That's one superpower of an underdog— setting up the conditions for people to root more intensely and excitedly for you, in the same way they might cheer for an underdog sports team. While in the first instance being under-estimated isn't flattering, if it's going on, you might as well take advantage of the clamor when you perform brilliantly (as you already knew you were capable of doing).

An underdog who achieves is awarded at least a temporary halo, which brings attention and an acceleration of support—including from those who didn't show confidence in the person before but now are rushing to join the winning side. If you're the lucky recip-ient of that attention, you'll likely feel a sense of pride and renewed energy. As a bonus, you'll have a compelling track record to point to when it comes to demonstrating other skills.

Perhaps most satisfyingly, when you win unexpected plaudits, there'll be a ripple effect. People will say, "I've heard good things about her," and "Isn't she the one who nailed the X account?" and "I'd love to work with her on my Y project."

Grace

When I was working at United Airlines as the chief procurement officer, United announced a merger with Continental Airlines. I was tapped to lead the integration plans across multiple corporate functions beyond my areas of expertise. This opportunity wouldn't have come my way had it not been for the equity I'd built in the company by transforming the organization's effectiveness. In the end, the teams I led designed new organization structures, selected optimal talent for key roles, defined best processes, and completed an analysis to not just meet but exceed the synergies expected of the merger.

Superpower: Confidence

Both of us learned early on that even when others underestimate us, we should never underestimate ourselves. We urge you to actively work on developing that inner confidence. If you're confident in yourself, even in an environment where others may be misjudging or underestimating you, that is another superpower, because you're quite aware that you can do better, that you can do more, that you can perform outside your box. Knowing it, you can be very intentional about how you demonstrate it. Think of confidence as the propeller that drives you forward through sludgy water. It's something you can build intentionally along the way, by choosing to trust yourself in challenging situations.

According to a study published in *The Journal of Neuroscience*, our brains are biologically conditioned to be influenced by confident people.[7] If you project confidence, that superpower can overwhelm the bias signals that place you in the underdog camp.

Confidence is the characteristic that inspires you to reach higher and to remain undaunted, even when conditions are tough. Imagine how many of the leaders you want to emulate took this same journey, using an inner confidence to get them over the barriers.

Superpower: Motivation

Although you probably wouldn't choose to be an underdog in the workplace, it can be very motivating to come from behind and prove yourself. In fact, research has shown that having a slight perceived disadvantage is sometimes correlated with better outcomes. In a study of several decades of NBA and NCAA basketball games, researchers found that teams that were down by one point at the half were more likely to win the game.[8] This was shocking to a lot of people in the sports world, where any kind of disadvantage is typically seen as just that—a disadvantage. But the reasoning behind the results is simple: teams that were slightly behind at the half leveraged the underdog mindset, and this extra motivation made the difference.

Wharton professor Samir Nurmohamed, who has done extensive research on adversity in the workplace, has found that underdog expectations can lead to better performance and exceptionally high motivation. Writing for the *Harvard Business Review*, Nurmohamed cited many examples,[9] including Aly Raisman, a three-time Olympic gold medalist in gymnastics, who defied commentators' analysis that she was too old to succeed at her last Olympics. Raisman observed: "It's obviously not something that people expected or that's easy to do after you're taking a year off or having it be the second Olympics or being the 'Grandma' or whatever they like to say. So, I'm happy I proved everyone wrong."

Nurmohamed conducted a lab experiment with 156 business school students, to find out whether motivation to prove others wrong led to high performance in underdogs. He asked the students to complete a negotiations simulation. Before they started, he announced that researchers had made predictions on the likelihood of their negotiating effectively, assigning them categories— underdog, high expectations, or neutral expectations.

After the students performed the negotiations, researchers asked them questions about their designations, their desire to prove others wrong, their self-confidence, and their assertiveness. Nurmohamed found that those with underdog expectations performed better than either of the two other groups. He concluded that the desire to prove others wrong was the greatest motivating factor, as opposed to other motivations.

Nurmohamed recommends: "If you want to stay motivated in the face of underdog expectations, you need to think about why those expectations aren't credible. Consider why observers who see you as an underdog might not have an accurate picture of how effective you are or why you can be successful. If you are the leader, you want to make sure your employees know that *you think others' low expectations are not credible.*"

Christiana

My first year in consulting, I was assigned mostly to process improvement studies. When I had my annual review, the senior partner said, "The partners are concerned about your ability to do heavy quantitative analysis." Well, I wasn't surprised that they were concerned. They hadn't assigned me to do any! Any question about my capabilities was going to slow down my promotion to manager—whether that question stemmed from my actual performance or lack of opportunity. Fair or not, I knew that I would have to prove myself, so I asked for my next assignment to feature heavy quantitative modeling. The partners agreed, and on my next project I successfully led one of the most complex regression analyses possible. I knew I could figure it out, and I did. After that, no one questioned my quantitative capabilities.

Of course, it's not just the motivation to prove others wrong that can motivate an underdog. The satisfaction of achievement, the acknowledgment of superiors and peers, and the new opportunities that come with success are all motivational as well. But from a superpower standpoint, harnessing some of that competitive spirit can put you in a mental state to hit one out of the park.

Superpower: Resilience

We consider resilience one of the greatest superpowers of all. We're talking about developing muscles that will activate in challenging situations. Think of it as muscle memory kicking into action. With that capability to draw on, your job will be a lot easier. And as your confidence grows, you'll feel less pressure to constantly prove yourself to everyone around you.

As you level up, we urge you not to lose the underdog's mindset. Because resilience builds character, you'll feel even more acutely a sense of immense gratification after a job well done.

EXERCISE: BUILD YOUR SUPERPOWER MUSCLES

1. Be the confidence builder.
Let's say you're in line for a new opportunity at work and need to build your inner confidence. Take a tactical approach, which will prepare you to come to an interview from a position of strength.

Make a list of the inner qualities that make you a good candidate, such as being collaborative, tenacious, or hardworking.

Make a list of the practical qualities that make you a good candidate, such as specific experience or training.

Make a list of your relevant experience, including similar types of experience in unrelated jobs.

Answer the question: Why am I the best candidate for the job?

2. Stage a surprise.
Surprise can have a career-altering effect in that it jolts your superiors out of their assumptions. When the time is right, perform in a way that is unexpected: show your boss a professional paper you're writing for a peer review journal, give a compelling reason why you should be assigned to a project you weren't on the list for, sign up on your own for an online class on an advanced aspect of your profession—and so on. You can try this out with your boss, clients, or peers, highlighting whatever skill sets you want to be known for, but the real advantage comes from the expectations-breaking nature of your surprise.

3. Never play the underdog card.
It's one thing to benefit from the underdog edge.
It's quite another thing to *play* the underdog card.
When people feel insecure—especially early in their
careers—every mistake can feel like a calamity, and
every extra demand can feel overwhelming. There's a
temptation to make excuses: *I wasn't told . . . No one
gave me the chance . . . The tech was down . . . He
didn't return my call . . . I thought Kevin was taking
care of that.* You get the picture. Rather than getting
you off the hook, excuses undermine your efforts
to appear professional and competent. In the next
chapter we'll give you the tools to help you reverse
the situation or use it as a lesson for the next time.

KEY TAKEAWAYS

- Everyone is an underdog at some point in
  their careers.

- Being underestimated can actually be a big advantage.

- Confidence is the critical superpower.

- Leverage the momentum that comes from
  beating expectations.

6

Steer into the SKID

If everything seems under control, you're not going fast enough.

—Mario Andretti

I f you've ever driven on ice or snow, you know what it feels like to lose control. One minute you're cruising along thinking about your next vacation, and the next minute you're sliding sideways toward another car. Even a two-second fishtail can feel like a lifetime when you're no longer in control. In those moments of panic, it can be hard to know what to do, but if you hark back to driver's training, the advice has always been to steer into the skid. This means if your car swerves to the right, you turn the wheel to the right, even if every instinct screams for you to rotate it in the opposite direction. The goal is to align your tires, so they work together, putting you back on track.

When it comes to navigating your career, the same logic applies. Everyone hits a skid sometimes, no matter how good they are at what they do. Even outstanding performers experience periods of instability when it feels like everything is going sideways. The slump can be self-inflicted or the result of a change at work. It can be traceable to a cantankerous new boss or a mismatch in team values. Our advice when this inevitably happens? Steer into the SKID, the same way you'd react if your car hit an icy patch on the road. This reaction helps you straighten out and avoid the crash. By reacting strategically and aligning your efforts with the direction things are heading, you can stop a career skid, regain control, and build your professional resilience. Better yet, if you sense conditions becoming hazardous, you can take action to prevent a skid from happening.

For Christiana, this moment occurred when she was up for partnership at McKinsey. At a consulting firm, partnership is the currency of success. Each potential partner receives careful consideration from an evaluator, typically a partner from outside the candidate's office, who interviews their team, office leadership, and clients. To become a partner, you need to be elected by a global partner committee, which strongly considers the evaluator's recommendation. There are roughly three shots at election, typically starting around your sixth year at the firm. The harsh reality is that if you don't get elected in one of these rounds, you're permanently stalled. Most people leave the company when that happens.

Two years earlier, Christiana had reduced her hours to part time, and she knew it was a risk to continue this schedule during her "election window." Every senior partner in her office advised her to return to full time to be considered for election. Her evaluator echoed that advice.

Part time meant she worked four days a week instead of five. That extra day at home made life more enjoyable for her and her family because she could count on being in town at least three days a week. It meant she could volunteer in her son's preschool classroom and accompany him to important doctor's appointments.

That one-day-shorter workweek was perceived as radical at the time. However, the flexibility worked beautifully for Christiana. Going back to full time wasn't an option she wanted to consider, even if it improved her partner election chances. If she had been commanded to go back to full time, she knew she'd have left McKinsey entirely.

The first election round came. Christiana's phone rang. Her office manager was calling with bad news. The new partner list had gone out by email to all employees, and her name wasn't on it. Christiana wasn't completely surprised, since she was the first part-timer to be assessed for partnership, and only one of two potential partners in the entire firm working part time. She still had two more rounds and felt confident about the strength of her performance and client relationships.

What surprised her was the reaction of her colleagues. For days, her phone rang with one consolation call after another. People wanted to know if she was okay and said they felt sorry for her. The conventional wisdom was that her career at the firm was pretty much over. It was uncomfortable, to say the least, to be pitied by peers and viewed as a failure.

Christiana decided to stop explaining the situation to well-meaning colleagues and focus on the feedback from the evaluation committee. She not only studied the report but read between the lines, embracing the feedback fully instead of using her part-time status as the sole reason she didn't make partner. She soon came to see the critique as a gift. It was as if someone had given her a detailed game plan for how she could create more equity and impact.

Even with her increased efforts, the second round came and again she was passed over. By that point she felt somewhat anxious, but she was still comfortable in her choice to pursue her current path. Because she'd built her career on a solid foundation, she knew that whatever happened, she'd still be able to support her family and thrive. Meanwhile, looking ahead to the third round, she doubled down on developing additional opportunities. She conducted new research, published articles, and spoke at industry events to boost her reputation. These were all the things that anyone hoping to get elected would do.

When the third round came and she was elected partner, she was elated, and she also felt vindicated in the choice she'd made. Instead of giving in to the pressure to return to full time to improve her election chances, she was glad she'd stuck to her guns—even when colleagues thought her career was in a tailspin. Not only did she continue to thrive at McKinsey, but she treasured the extra time with her young son. No one since has ever remembered or asked why it took her seven years instead of six to get elected.

The SKID Discipline

When you hit an icy patch in a professional situation, be it with your boss, a colleague, a client, or a direct report, your brain kicks into high gear. Because experience has programmed it to halt upon detecting danger, your first instinct might be to slam on the proverbial brakes. To counteract this effectively, you must train yourself to recognize when circumstances require you to change your response. You can anticipate the skid and train yourself to recalibrate quickly.

We call this discipline SKID, and it applies to almost any career problem you may encounter. The four SKID steps include:

> **S**elf-assess.
> **K**eep your power.
> **I**ncrease equity.
> **D**eliver performance.

By following these steps, you can take a proactive stance toward situations that feel unmanageable and keep your efforts from spinning wildly off target. Not only will they make your reactions more effective, but they will also reduce your stress and anxiety because the SKID discipline gives you clarity of thought and action, ultimately leading you to better decisions for yourself and your career.

Step 1. Self-assess.

When something happens that lets you know you're dealing with a potential skid, we urge you to take a pragmatic rather than emotional approach. It's completely natural to feel upset and disappointed when something doesn't go your way, but you can't enter into battle every time your feelings are hurt or you're disappointed. It's not that we're saying, "Suck it up!" Far from it. The key is to respond with self-awareness and emotional intelligence as you take concrete steps to assess the best way forward. To this end, you must know the difference between responses that are merely ego-driven and those that are Career Forward.

We both have encountered slights and insults that made us feel bad but had nothing to do with our ability to build equity at work and create an impact. Making that distinction is critical. If a slight doesn't diminish your equity, there's no value in personalizing the issue. For example, if your boss invites your male peers to sporting events and not you, move on, even if it bothers you.

However, if the slight materially diminishes your ability to contribute, then you owe it to yourself and your company to address the issue. Having worked in numerous companies and business environments and having gone through plenty of mergers, acquisitions, and leadership changes, we've seen countless skids happen to people. When the ground starts to shift under you, it can take you by surprise. This often happens when your company or unit merges with another, when the company strategy shifts dramatically, when new leadership takes over, and sometimes when you least expect it. When a good performer encounters a problem, it means something has changed in the environment and it's up to the affected person to diagnose and address it.

When Grace was at United Airlines, she had an experience with a new company hire who was very smart but was having trouble earning the support of her team. Grace observed that this new hire was overconfident about the procurement methods she'd mastered at a previous automotive company, and she was frustrated that her airline team members weren't getting on board. They struggled to understand the new processes and didn't see the advantages over what they were already doing.

One evening this woman came by Grace's office to vent about how slow the team was in adopting her new model. She clearly believed that she was in the right, and the issue was how to force more cooperation. After listening to her, Grace suggested that she think about the situation from her team's perspective. Maybe the slow adoption was due to her team's not understanding the new processes. Did they have the financial acumen to run the new models, or did they need training? Had she shared success stories that might motivate them to make the change? Was she conscious about acknowledging the differences between the automobile industry and the airline industry? Once Grace's new colleague began to shift her thinking and focus on training and motivating the team by celebrating successful outcomes, the results came. This approach transformed a skid moment in her leadership to a productive new path at the company.

If you're struggling and experiencing a skid, instead of making assumptions, step back and self-assess. Take an objective look at your performance and your environment. Note that human nature and social norms in work settings may make it hard to get a good read on the situation. Colleagues tend to be polite to one another and nonconfrontational. Even if your coworkers notice something amiss, they might not tell you. People tend to be guarded with this kind of feedback because they don't want to create problems or damage relationships. That's why the likelihood of being told flat out that you're starting to skid is low. Instead, you need to get good at reading the signals.

To do this, reflect on your recent interactions. Some common tells can indicate to you that others are withdrawing their engagement and support for you and your projects. Pay attention to them. People are uncannily good at picking up when a person is losing equity or influence and may separate themselves from the person. If you see your colleagues begin to distance themselves from you, stop and reflect on why it might be happening.

Here are some signs that you're heading into a skid at work. How many apply to you?

- You aren't invited to meetings that you used to attend or that your peers are attending.
- You have trouble getting others to join special projects you've been asked to lead.
- Your colleagues don't seek your opinion or feedback.
- Colleagues who have similar tenure and performance records are getting promoted faster than you.
- A new position has been added above yours. Although your title is the same, you've effectively been brought down a level in the organization chart.

- You have a hard time getting one-on-one time with your boss.
- You feel out of the loop when it comes to communication.
- When colleagues praise one another in meetings or on your company's message board, your name doesn't come up.
- Your performance review scores have been declining.
- Your last raise or bonus was lower than expected.
- You realize that you no longer have supporters.

Christiana

When I was at Nike, I hired many people from outside the company to run our fast-growing direct-to-consumer business. One guy in particular had all the skills and experience needed for his role, but after the honeymoon of being the new guy wore off, he began experiencing difficulty getting the necessary support from his work peers. He had a sense that things weren't going well, but chalked it up to those colleagues "not getting" how his business operated. Once I realized he was starting to skid, I leaned in to help him listen to those colleagues, understand the (largely style-driven) issues he was confronting, and work in a focused way to build more effective relationships. The style adjustments he made allowed him to get back on an accelerated path.

The goal of stepping back and reflecting is to look at your situation as objectively as possible—to not let pride and hurt feelings cause you to act when you don't need to, or conversely, to pretend you don't have a problem when you do. If many of the statements above apply to you, ignoring the situation only makes it worse. Once you notice it, the next steps help you to understand why it's happening and take corrective actions.

Step 2. Keep your power.

Before you look outside for solutions, ask yourself what *you* can do to improve your situation. Even when the root cause of the issue is far beyond your sphere of influence, you still have agency, and putting the ball back in your court not only feels empowering but has a tangible benefit. The more proactive you feel, the stronger you'll be. Conversely, a sense of helplessness can spiral, blinding you to constructive actions. Keep reminding yourself that you always have power to act, no matter how helpless you may feel in the moment. This is the mentality you must have to prevail.

If you're at a loss about where to start, turn to people you trust for advice and perspective. Think of them as your Trust Circle. Ask mentors and close peers for input, especially those who understand your team, the environment, and work processes, and who have your best interests at heart. Let them know they should speak frankly and constructively. Prepare to be open and remind yourself that these trusted souls are there to help you. Your best allies are people who believe in you and want you to succeed. Candid feedback is the best gift. Even if you disagree with what people in your Trust Circle are telling you, keep the conversation positive and constructive. Aim for questions that will give you concrete feedback.

Instead of asking, "How can I improve?" ask, "How can I run the project/lead meetings/engage with peers more effectively?"

Instead of asking, "How am I doing?" ask, "If you had one piece of advice that would help me take my performance to the next level, what would it be?"

The group is there to help you identify blind spots. For example, a woman Christiana mentored was overwhelmed by her workload even as her boss kept adding more and more projects. The woman appealed to Christiana for advice. Christiana helped her realize she had a choice of either letting her performance slip (not ideal) or choosing to assert herself with her boss (not easy, but more likely to succeed). When she recognized her power in the situation, the woman summoned the courage to speak with her boss and told him candidly about her work overload. He hadn't realized what was happening, and he responded well, resolving the problem and helping her prioritize.

Maybe your boss values certain qualities that aren't spelled out but are implicit. In every organization, a favored group inevitably rises to prominence. These individuals get pulled into exciting strategic initiatives and work situations. Everyone seems to want their opinions, and everything they touch succeeds. Who are those favored people at your organization? Why have they earned so much clout? By identifying and studying the rising stars, you can uncover the elements driving their success. Maybe your new boss makes bold decisions and likes those who do the same, making your careful, analytical approach no longer the asset it once was. This insight can provide valuable information.

EXERCISE: CREATE YOUR OWN ASSESSMENT TOOL

Many companies offer an evaluation process to help employees identify strengths and areas for improvements. If you don't have access to a formal assessment, don't worry. You don't have to rely on HR. Instead, create your own evaluation by asking colleagues and clients for constructive feedback about yourself. Let them know the responses will be seen only by you with the sole purpose of self-improvement. The trick is to keep it short and simple. Because there's no need to tabulate responses for multiple people, we suggest you use open-ended questions and keep them short and specific so that respondents need no more than five to ten minutes to respond. Here are some general questions you can tailor to the specific areas you want to develop:

What is one thing I can do to strengthen your confidence in me to accomplish my job?

What do you most appreciate about working with me?

What are three or four words you'd use to describe my interaction with others?

What is one thing I should start doing to be a more effective leader?

What is one thing I should stop doing to be a more effective leader?

Write down the answers and revisit them every so often, to be sure you're staying on track.

Step 3. Increase your equity.

As we described in chapter 3, building career equity is the key to long-term success. Don't forget your equity when you're in a skid. Take a Career Forward approach. Rather than focus on the unfairness of your boss or the situation, zero in on the elements within your control that can increase your ability to create value for your company.

Christiana remembers a situation when she was a new consulting manager, working with a leading global retailer. The company had recently brought in a new CEO, and Christiana had focused on building a strong relationship with him, knowing it would help her and the team have more impact. Along the way, the partner on the project (Christiana's boss) asked her to bring him along to her regular check-ins with the CEO. Her boss was struggling to build his own connection with the CEO and wanted to leverage what Christiana had built. The challenge was that the CEO had told Christiana in the past that he didn't like her boss and wasn't interested in spending time with him.

As the more junior person, Christiana was in a bind. She ultimately conceded and brought her boss to the next CEO check-in, and the meeting was a flat-out disaster. The discussion was awkward, the CEO wouldn't speak frankly, and her boss didn't make a positive impression. There were repercussions, too. The CEO canceled their check-ins for the remainder of the project, and Christiana and the team had to do a lot of "repair work" to gain the CEO's support for their recommendations. Christiana learned an important lesson from this painful skid: once you've built personal equity, you need to *protect* it to continue to grow as a professional.

Step 4. Deliver performance.

The last step of the SKID discipline echoes our evergreen advice for the book, which is to excel at your job. You need to be so good at what you do that you can choose to work anywhere. When the road feels especially treacherous, make doubly sure you do your work well. If anything, step up your game. Remind people of your value while you figure out your next step. Don't become a target by giving anyone reason to question your work product. Do everything you can to help your team succeed. Be professional, honest, and clear.

Although you need to manage your reactions, it doesn't mean you should be passive, especially when it comes to protecting your ability to do your job.

Grace's career path got a bit slippery when she found herself working for yet another new boss. This was her third boss in approximately four years. You know how it is when a new leader comes in. They bring their own norms and expectations and expect everyone to adjust to these. The new boss gravitated toward Grace's colleague, who, like him, had been with the company for years and shared a love of golfing. Hearing them talk about their golf weekend scores and tell inside jokes about past shared experiences, Grace, who was fairly new to the company, felt out of the loop. Nevertheless, she pushed aside her unease and focused on delivering strong results.

When it came time to craft her team's strategic plan, Grace took the opportunity to shine. She encouraged the team to stretch its goals and adapt to promising opportunities that she believed were not only doable but necessary for the company's growth. When she received the agenda for the team's presentation to the CEO and executive team, Grace noticed that she and her peer shared the same slot, which allowed barely enough time to cover both their areas of responsibility. Her boss must have had the same concern, because on the evening before the presentation, he came to her office. "It's going to be a tight schedule," he said. "Why don't you email your presentation to the group instead of attending? That way, they can read all the important details when they have time."

Grace was confused. She knew the decision couldn't have been about her performance, since she was delivering strong results and getting great feedback. She finally concluded that her boss, in wanting to make the best use of the time, had given her peer a leg up because of their easy relationship. Whether her boss acted consciously or not, it put her at a disadvantage.

Grace thought long and hard about how she should respond, and by the time she went to bed that night, she had her answer.

She knew that skipping the presentation would put her strategic plan at risk because it required her to align with the executive team on the investments and deliverables over the next five years. She also knew that attending would require answering strategic questions during the meeting to ensure everyone's full understanding and support. She decided the work was too important to avoid the opportunity to interact strategically with senior leadership. This was a moment for her to show up.

When her cell phone alarm went off on the morning of the presentation, Grace discovered that her husband had changed the ringtone to the theme from *Rocky*. It made her laugh and gave her just the boost of humor and inspiration she needed. Jumping out of bed, she put on her sharpest suit and headed to the office.

The first to arrive, she secured one of the few seats in the conference room and waited for the rest of the leadership team. When her boss walked in, he did a double take. "Oh, Grace, you are here?" She replied, "Yep, I'm excited and ready to share my team's strategic plan." She smiled as if their conversation the previous evening had never occurred. As she took her place at the executive conference table, she realized, based on the reactions of others, that no one else knew her boss had recommended she skip this critical meeting to save time for her male peer to present.

When it was her turn to present, the months of preparation paid off. As expected, the senior team had lots of questions, which Grace handled with confidence, since she knew the details of the plan backward and forward. From that day on, her boss treated her with new respect.

If you feel out of favor at the moment, remember that this dynamic can change, sometimes quite drastically. When a new senior leader comes in, they often build their team with people they know and relate to from past roles. This shakes up the status quo and can shift the company culture if a significant number of leadership positions turn over. The same kind of thing also happens during a merger or acquisition, with the larger company's culture generally eclipsing the smaller company's culture. When the culture of the company or most of the talent changes, the inner circle also changes. These are times to be especially alert and proactive. Sometimes this simply means being more conscious about interacting with certain people and building new relationships. Don't be intimidated. Reach out to colleagues, especially new ones, and see how you can support them. Often people from different backgrounds can find common ground to bond; usually it just takes time.

Don't drain your energies by getting caught in a cycle of resentment. After all, the person most hurt by negative emotions is you. Optimism will help you be resilient through change. This is the perfect time to remember that your job is not your career. A setback in your job doesn't have to translate to your career. If you focus on your Career Forward goals, you'll be able to stay agile and adjust your approach to remain effective.

In the end, it's helpful to keep things in perspective. Know that everyone skids at one time or another. Remind yourself of that when you're feeling uncertain. Some people seem to have a natural ability to let the hard times roll off them. Watch what they do. Grace has a friend, Ellen, who is like that. She'll look at a calamity and say, "Boy, there are some days when no matter who you are, it's coming down on you." She'll laugh in the face of a calamity, while everyone around her is pulling their hair out, and respond, "It's kind of funny. It's kind of interesting, isn't it?" She has a talent for keeping calm and carrying on, and this ability can be invaluable. But it doesn't necessarily happen automatically. Think of it as a conscious choice and develop a mechanism to help you stay centered. Maybe you achieve calmness by reflecting on your place in the world and on what you can and cannot control—or maybe by learning to focus your attention on productive action. By doing that, you keep the noise and the drama in the background.

A final thought. We each experienced some tough times in our careers. We both dealt with turnarounds. During those times we'd think, *This is really hard!* But interestingly, we were simultaneously experiencing feelings of intense immersion and thinking, *Wow, this is a great experience, and I'm going to tough it out—and it will be worth it.* Even when work is tough, if it's meaningful it can be exhilarating, and the idea that you can solve a big problem is exciting. Make career skids serve a purpose.

If you're a high performer, you're going to have a long career journey, with many ups and downs. Just remember: resiliency and confidence are built every time you steer through the skids and take back control of your career progression.

KEY TAKEAWAYS

- Learn to spot the early signs of career skid. When things go sideways, be strategic.

- If things go sideways, stay in the tension and work the problem.

- Let failure—and feedback from wise colleagues— teach you.

- Be willing to move on if you can't get back on track.

7

What Makes You Special?

Building a brand means knowing your story
and building and sharing that story.
—Tamara McCleary, CEO Thulium

What's your secret sauce—your professional brand, the "it factor" that sets you apart and makes you shine?

You might cringe at hearing more talk of brands; it's easy to think of *brand* as a costume you wear for the public eye. While it's true that some people love the whirl of networking at industry conferences and engaging on social media—and they have a knack for displaying their accomplishments whenever they get a chance—when we talk about your professional brand, we're referring to a deeper concept built around your authentic self in the workplace: what makes you the distinctive professional you are.

The key question is how to put yourself out there in a way that benefits both you and your company. A Career Forward view will help you manage your exposure in a way that broadens your self-esteem and impact. It will help you avoid the superficial elements of branding, the time-sucking focus on self-promotion, and the tendency to celebrate "shiny pennies" over substantive achievements.

We're not denying that reputation matters—indeed, it's crucial. While it would be great if all you had to do was perform well in your current role to craft the most distinctive career identity, we've learned you must be much more intentional and strategic to develop an image with your peers that truly supports your career goals. Few companies (or business programs) teach employees the best ways to build their professional brands, so the two of us had to learn by doing. We watched colleagues who'd built powerful reputations and people who seemed to have huge personal networks, and we learned that at its most fundamental, your personal brand starts with what differentiates you.

The Professional Differentiator

As you move through your career, you'll find that there are plenty of competent people who can perform on the job. That's true no matter how high you go. Excelling is important, but here we're looking a step beyond, asking you to consider, in addition to doing well in your field, what extra something you bring to the table that differentiates you. Think of it as your trademark.

Your trademark can be anything from a special skill that's unusual in your field to a personal quality that makes you stand out. It's the yellow highlight around your name that is memorable to others. As you look at your career over the long term, it will be helpful to identify that trademark and build on it as your professional life develops.

Christiana

Four years into working in consulting, I took an in-town assignment that enabled me to spend more time with my son after maternity leave. That was how I discovered my love for the retail industry. It was unlike anything I'd done before, and I found it fascinating. I became intentional about continuously developing my knowledge of retail, staying abreast of trends, and writing articles to share my thoughts on everything from merchandising to the supply chain.

At McKinsey, it was always a priority to share knowledge and best practices to build on one another's work and help each other, so I volunteered to speak about the retail industry at our internal conferences. I became known as "the "Retail Queen" in my firm. If my colleagues had questions about retail or if any new opportunities in this area came up, they thought of me. This served me well, because it positioned me for the kind of work I enjoyed and helped me further build out my experience. Years later, my strong background in consulting in the retail industry was a key factor in transitioning to a senior role at Nike.

Over time, the value of this conscious branding will become obvious. Once you reach a certain point in your career, you'll have other people around you who are also good at their jobs and shine in various ways. Some will have a job-first mentality and will be less interested in networking or defining themselves in an intentional way in their professional community. Your clarity about your differentiators will give you an advantage.

When you're thinking about how to define your professional brand or trademark, you can begin by asking yourself, *What would people in my profession say about me?* For example:

"She's fast on her feet."

"She understands the technical details and can explain them clearly in terms people understand."

"She's the first person who comes to mind when we need a problem solver."

"She's super smart and intuitive."

"She knows how to mobilize teams."

"She's got great people skills."

"She attracts top talent to work with her."

"She always gets the job done."

Having a positive reputation helps you gain clout, gives you a better chance at getting chosen for special assignments, and can fast-track you for internal promotions or job offers outside of your company. But in addition to being seen in a positive way, you also want to be known as an expert in a certain niche to add value to your brand. There are countless ways people hone their professional brand, but a lot of times it comes down to trying something new—discovering an interest or talent and then leaning into it.

Your Brand Strategy

To be strategic about your professional brand, you must first be strategic about your work. The more experience you gain in specific areas, the better you'll understand how your skills and passions set you apart. From there, you can work to go deep, sharpen your capabilities, and leverage communications channels in your company to share stories of your impact. Over time, you'll become known as the resident expert for the specific work you love. Digital marketing guru Krista Neher has said the following about building a successful digital brand: "Start by knowing what you want and who you are, build credibility around it, and deliver it [online] in a compelling way." In our experience, that same philosophy can be applied to building your personal brand. While developing a strong professional brand *within* your organization may happen naturally over time, we still recommend you approach it with intent. More difficult is developing a reputation outside of your organization.

You want to get noticed in your industry for the right reasons and to make new connections that could benefit you both in the present and in the future. To do this, you'll need to consider how to get yourself out there—and how often. If you set your sights too low, you could miss out on exciting possibilities, but if you try to do too much, you could develop a reputation for being preoccupied with self-promotion. Like so many things, it's a balancing act.

The construction of an external reputation is an important aspect of personal brand strategy. Many of us often underestimate the need to be proactive and deliberate when it comes to nurturing our networks. Early in their careers in particular, women may not devote as much effort as they should to cultivating their personal brands outside of their current employers, especially when they have a lot of demands on their time already. Work can be all-consuming, and if you tack on family commitments and personal obligations, there isn't usually a lot of time left over. When women invest so much in their jobs and families, they often miss out on making new connections outside their organizations. This can set them back when it comes to scouting out job prospects and gaining recognition in their industry.

Never underestimate the power of building your network, both inside and outside your organization. If you don't cultivate your network, your under-connectedness can end up becoming a limiting factor in finding new opportunities. Make network cultivation an intentional scheduled activity.

For instance, Christiana used to put tickler reminders in her calendar to prompt her to stay in touch on a regular basis with existing contacts (including past colleagues). Use this kind of simple intentional strategy to seek out new relationships, whether with the clients you serve or people you meet at industry events. Send them an article, ask them to lunch, or see if they want to hop on a video call to catch up. Getting to know people and staying in touch with them will benefit both you and your organization. You might hear of someone who is looking for a job and would be the perfect fit at your company, or you might learn about an open position that's exactly what you've been looking for. The more you do this, the more natural it gets—and the more people you know, the more opportunities you'll have.

Consider the channels and outlets that can help you. When we talk about brand-building exposure, we're referring to anything that's related to your job and connects you with people outside your company in a professional capacity—but that isn't typically part of your official job description. These undertakings are akin to extracurricular activities back in school; though they aren't required, they *are* enriching and rewarding and can benefit you for years to come.

Here are some examples:

- Joining industry associations, professional organizations, or nonprofits.
- Speaking at industry or professional association events.
- Attending conferences and networking events.
- Writing articles or books.
- Maintaining a presence on social media channels (e.g., LinkedIn) and posting about industry topics.
- Having a professional website/blog.
- Cultivating a professional email list.
- Hosting a podcast or being a podcast guest.
- Doing interviews with media outlets.

You certainly don't need to leverage all these strategies, but it's good to know that you have a multitude of options to consider. Participating in external reputation-building activities can provide a tangible boost to your long-term prospects. Not only will you learn more and flex new muscles that you don't typically use on a day-to-day basis, but you'll beef up your résumé and professional network. In the process you'll join the social mix of individuals who go above and beyond what's required in their roles, expanding your professional circle to include the top tier of industry peers.

Grace

As a Cuban American and one of a relatively small number of women executives in the upper reaches of the Fortune 500, I was asked throughout my career to represent the companies that I worked for at external and internal forums devoted to diversity and inclusion. I considered that speaking and engagement part of my corporate leadership responsibility. Of course, it benefited my company and our employees, but it built my personal brand as well.

The Right Backing

No matter what your reputation-building goals are, you want to make sure your company supports your activities. It's essential that what you're doing outside of your full-time role not constitute a conflict of interest. Luckily, getting support from your employer should be doable if you have the right strategy. First, it's important to understand why your company might not want you to be in the spotlight.

The most obvious reason is that it could be a distraction from your work. For example, if you're attending industry events that occur during regular business hours, it's easy to see how that might conflict with other priorities.

Another issue employers tend to be concerned about is company privacy. Sharing too much information is something that competitors can use to their advantage. There's a legitimate worry that employees in public forums could accidentally divulge confidential information.

Depending on who you work for, you might face resistance in getting approval for an activity that would put you in the spotlight. On the flip side, you might find yourself with a great deal of autonomy. Either way, it's essential that you speak directly with relevant leadership to communicate your plans and get approval before you ramp up efforts to get exposure. Since there are obvious risks associated with allowing employees to build their personal brand outside of work, many companies will take a conservative position on the matter unless the employee comes to the table ready to articulate the benefits. It's on you to show that the activity is a win-win for you and the company both.

Christiana

When I was at Nike, the company was understandably cautious about sharing what was going on inside, so employee public speaking opportunities were typically limited. I understood that perspective, but I also saw a downside. By keeping a very low profile, we weren't catching the eye of top talent in retail/digital who could potentially be interested in working on my team. I realized that getting more exposure within the industry could help fill our pipeline with quality hires. After all, the people we wanted to meet stayed abreast of what was happening in the industry by regularly attending events and reading articles. If we were actively participating in those forums, we could connect with more people directly.

So I explained to leadership that I wanted to speak at and attend conferences on a very selective basis. I worked with the communications team to identify the most relevant, high-profile speaking opportunities, and I took media training to be sure I could deliver our messages effectively. I also committed to going out of my way to make new connections that could potentially fill our pipeline, making sure I delivered on my promise of tying clear benefits back to the organization. When I demonstrated success, I was rewarded with more opportunities. In the end, it truly was a win-win.

Striking the Exposure Balance

In the early years of your career, it can be difficult to get high-quality exposure opportunities. You'll need to start small and focus on building your experience and confidence. But the more well-known and successful you become, the less you'll have to push yourself out there to get opportunities. Instead, you'll begin to experience a pull from the market. You may be asked to be the keynote speaker at conferences, a guest on podcasts, or an invited expert in front of university classes. At first this can be a nice change of pace because it's easier than chasing those kinds of leads on your own. Interesting opportunities may fall into your lap from out of nowhere, and you'll be able to accommodate most.

But it's important to be selective about how many invitations you choose to accept. Your time is valuable, and you don't want to compromise your regular work commitments or obligations in your personal life. So make sure you set boundaries. You're at risk when either of the following occurs:

Your company is overpromoting you. Proud of your success as a woman, your company might favor you for public-facing opportunities. Their objective is to show people outside the company that it's a place where women can excel. That's generally a good thing, because it gives you an opportunity to build your experience and personal brand. But if the company uses you in this role too often, it can reduce the time available to manage your regular responsibilities. If this happens, don't be afraid to speak up and get the balance right.

You're overpromoting yourself. Not only can overexposure become a distraction from your core work responsibilities, but it can also end up hurting your reputation. People might get the impression that you're all about building your personal brand, rather than doing a good job in your full-time role and helping your organization. Stay humble and focused on your professional contributions, and you'll avoid having your external activities backfire on you.

Handling a "Shiny Penny"

We all know that person. The colleague who's all shine and little substance is a familiar character in most workplaces, and as you rise to more senior levels, you may find yourself competing with him or her for plum assignments or promotions.

It can be frustrating, since these people often don't have much to offer behind the flash. Shiny pennies spend disproportionate amounts of time on self-promotion. Since they generate attention, onlookers will tend to pay close attention to what they say and show eagerness to ingratiate themselves with them. A natural instinct may be to attach yourself to a colleague who is "going places," but pay attention to whether they're really contributing. The shiny penny colleague will typically be nowhere to be found when it comes to the nitty-gritty of work deliverables.

How do you handle a shiny penny? Better still, how do you turn a shiny penny to your advantage?

Christiana once worked with such a person. Mike [not his real name] had it all. He was handsome, charming, whip-smart, and a dynamo on the speaker's circuit. When Mike walked into a room, everyone looked in his direction, like plants turning toward the sun.

But when Christiana worked with Mike on projects, it was a challenge for her because she was focused on substance and Mike seemed to succeed with appearances. What could she do? Her approach was strategic:

Christiana

First, I kept delivering the goods to ensure that my business was performing. Second, I made a conscious decision not to engage. I wasn't going to spend any time in meetings brooding on what he was doing and how I was the one delivering the goods. I said to myself, *I understand what's going on here, but I'm not going to give it my energy.* Nor was I going to acknowledge or get sucked into unproductive grievances.

The lesson here was one I learned from watching professional athletes: focus on the ball, not the player. If you have a situation where you're working with a shiny penny and you're spending all your time saying, "Oh my god, what are they doing? I can't believe it," you're not focusing on the ball.

Third, I lifted my game in a couple of areas where I realized I could take a page out of his book. Taking a step back, I was able to recognize that there were strategies he employed that could be helpful to me and that I could incorporate into my plan. For example, he always made an effort to interact with every person in the room. His social skills were top-notch. I realized I could take a few tips from that without compromising my authenticity.

Finally, I outwaited him, and he eventually flew too close to the sun and burned out, overcommitting resources to a project he championed that was not a success. I wouldn't wish failure on anyone, so my advice is to always make sure the substance matches the shine.

You've got to consciously decide how you're going to handle a shiny penny, because the phenomenon is not going away. During your career, you'll see these people overrated and promoted while others pick up after them and fix their failures. But you can't let that pull your energy from what really matters. Our advice is to focus on playing the game that *you* can win.

Create a Plan for Your Professional Brand

As your career develops and your goals evolve, you will need to be proactive about dialing your level of exposure up or down. Here are some tips that have worked well for us over the years.

- **Set goals:** It's helpful to develop metrics and stay true to them. For example, you can attend conferences relevant to your area of expertise. Begin with one a year and then increase your participation. Make sure you connect with interesting people at each event and keep their contact information. Many companies will cover the expenses for professional development events, which helps make this doable. As you get more senior, you might set a goal of publishing thought pieces on LinkedIn or writing articles for relevant trade journals. You might also target speaking at industry events. At each stage, when the year is over, you can assess your outcomes. Ask yourself questions like *What did I learn? How did I build my network contacts?* You can also evaluate how you want to dial things up or down from there.

- **Prioritize:** Don't accept every invitation just because you're invited. People with career equity are selective and choose the external engagements that offer the greatest value. Remember that the more your brand grows, the more people will want to use it for their benefit. They'll play to your ego, telling you how great you are and how much they'd love to have you involved. If you set boundaries early, it's easier to say no to opportunities that aren't a good fit.

- **Leverage your passions:** Don't just go through the motions; tap into your passions so that you enjoy yourself along the way. Get involved with organizations and causes that you feel strongly about, and make sure you're participating in a way that lights you up. If you love speaking, ramp up the keynotes. If you love writing, author more articles.

- **Make the most of your efforts:** When you carve out time for something, go all in. At conferences, that means planning to meet a certain number of new people each day and even doing your homework to set meetings with specific attendees in advance. When you're as strategic about your exposure as you'd be with a day spent at the office, you'll get the best outcomes.

Consider this exposure as an extension of your professional contribution, as well as a constant learning opportunity. It's a way to give back to others while also helping yourself. The more you interact with people externally and share with them, the more you expand your perspective. It's a win-win.

When it comes to managing your brand and professional exposure, it's all about thoughtful strategy. You should plan to dial things up or down as your bandwidth and interests change. You'll likely also need to flex your efforts and evolve your career identity over time as you advance. Above all, remember that though reputation building is an essential aspect of a successful career and can help open many doors, it never trumps how you perform in your day-to-day role.

KEY TAKEAWAYS

- Identify the qualities that make you different.
- Build a substantial professional reputation in your company and your field.
- Shine your light in a strategic and equity-building way.
- Learn how to handle distracting "shiny pennies" when they appear.

8

Your 360-Degree Life

According to LeanIn and McKinsey's latest study on women in the workplace, women in corporate America are burned out, with one in three considering leaving the workplace or down-shifting their careers.[1] The two of us love our work. The joy we take in what we do is a big part of our Career Forward mindset. So when the question arises as to how women can resolve the constant struggle between their work, family, and personal life, we tend to answer in a different way. We reject the portrayal of work and nonwork life as essentially facing off against each other. We think the question of how to achieve work/life balance is the wrong question. Instead, we propose a different model—managing what we call the 360-degree life.

The 360-degree life takes into account your whole self. It doesn't pit different arenas against each other, but, rather, helps you both succeed and be fulfilled. It's not that there aren't trade-offs—we all experience these. The point is not to hide all the things you have going on, whether it's work or working out, family or friends, your career or a separate passion that you want to pursue.

Back when we entered the workforce, the norm was for people to keep their personal and professional lives as separate as possible. This was especially true for women, who historically had borne the burden of being the primary caretakers for children. In most corporate suites, there was doubt about whether working mothers—or future mothers—could remain fully committed to the demands of their jobs and consistently progress in their careers. As she headed off on maternity leave, Christiana remembers a senior partner telling her, "We really do hope you'll come back," which was her first clue that many of the partners did not expect her to return. Another partner gave her a thick book on supply chain excellence as a baby shower gift, suggesting she read it while on leave, signaling that maternity leave was viewed as vacation time.

In the early years of our careers, we saw women being judged if they let their personal lives spill over into their work lives. It was common for working moms to devise coping techniques like leaving their jackets on the backs of chairs when they had to duck out for a child's appointment, so if anyone stopped by their desk, it looked like they were still around the office somewhere. Everyone knew these women had children, and at some point, those children would need their moms to take them to the doctor or attend important school events. But as normal an expectation as that was, it was almost taboo to openly speak about it at work. It was viewed as smarter and more strategic to say you had to leave the office to get some dental work done than to say you were leaving for a school conference, which is probably why women had so many dental appointments. We remember that it was often totally okay for a male colleague to step out to get a haircut, yet the mere mention by a female employee of "family appointments" was enough to call into question her commitment and put her performance under scrutiny.

During the early years of their careers, more women than ever were entering the workplace, but they were often heard to say they were working because they "had to." It was as if actually working because one loved it was tantamount to putting family responsibilities second, a choice that would have rubbed against the existing traditional biases of male colleagues.

Christiana remembers how conflicted she felt about going back to work when her son was three months old. Her first day back, she was at her desk and decided to walk to Starbucks and get a cup of coffee. She felt a small thrill that she could just get up and go. Then, later, she was standing in the hallway talking to her coworkers, and she experienced another thrill: *I'm talking to adults!* Many parents can relate to that feeling. It doesn't always get talked about, even today, but we're all complete human beings, and it's not just okay, it's *critical* to enjoy those different parts of ourselves to succeed in the long term.

Thankfully, social and professional norms have evolved over time, and forward-thinking companies are now encouraging their employees to bring their whole selves to work. Instead of sneaking around to care for a sick child, workers are generally able to be much more open about personal responsibilities that spill into the workday. The pandemic kicked this movement into high gear, as many people worked from home and the boundaries between their work life and their home life were visibly erased, courtesy of video meetings. COVID was devastating in many ways, but the silver lining for millions of working professionals was that companies had little choice but to offer their employees more flexibility in handling personal obligations. In the process, many employers have realized that this flexibility can have huge positive impacts on productivity, retention, and morale.

The reality of being a multifaceted human being—living a 360-degree life—is that work spills over into your personal life, and your personal life spills over into your professional life. The more successful you become, and the richer your personal life is, the more this happens. A Career Forward mindset means embracing the opportunity and owning the challenge of living a full life while building a rewarding, successful career.

So where do women stand today? Here we find both good news and bad news. There are more options for flexibility in today's workplace, including more control over time with remote work, flexible schedules, and collaboration technology. The evolution of company policies—along with changes in the culture and more openness in family roles—has also improved opportunities for women, although obvious gaps remain. For example, although unpaid parental leave is available for the majority of workers, according to one study, only 20 percent receive paid leave. (The Bureau of Labor Statistics put the number at 23 percent.)[2]

Many companies have improved their cultures to make them more supportive of women and families, but the reality on the ground is challenging. Nearly 12 million women left their jobs in the early months of the pandemic, primarily because kids weren't going to school and there was little childcare support available.[3] Obviously, this was an exceptional crisis, but it shined a light on just how vulnerable women in the workplace can be and how primary responsibility for children is still skewed disproportionately toward women.

The responsibility for improving how our personal life meshes with our work life, for creating and supporting solutions, rests with all of us: families, employees, employers, even government officials. But along with that, every woman must acquire the skills and gain the professional leverage to be a successful advocate for herself. Then we all can live our best 360-degree lives.

You Built Professional Equity—Now Use It

You'll be better positioned to attain a 360-degree life if you've accumulated professional equity. With that equity comes leverage—especially in an unusually competitive job market. The more incentivized your employer is to keep you, the more obtainable will be job concessions that support your career advancement and other life priorities. But you need to be smart about it and strategize what you want and need. Don't be afraid to draw down your equity a bit if you need to. That's why you built it up.

Christiana

When my son was little, I was traveling every other week and working long hours at McKinsey, and it was starting to wear me down. I tried to quit three times, but my mentor kept talking me out of it. Ideally, I wanted to have some kind of part-time arrangement, but even if the partners said yes, I feared it would kill my chances of advancing because it was believed that as a part-timer, it's harder to do high-impact work and remain a strategic player.

Figuring I had nothing to lose, I decided to propose a custom solution. I would temporarily switch to part time, working four days a week while keeping 80 percent of the workload and 80 percent of the pay. Much to my colleagues' surprise, McKinsey agreed to my suggestion. But they made it clear to me that this was a very temporary arrangement that should last only six to twelve months.

Needing to drop 20 percent of my workload, I decided to be strategic about how I did it. I wanted to continue being a revenue generator, because that's how people got elected to partner. So I prioritized everything on the client front and dropped other "unleveraged" work, such as recruiting at college campuses. Working 80 percent of my normal hours, I had to be especially protective of my time and focus on what mattered most.

My plan ended up working out just fine. Even though I was part time, I maintained relevancy with the top leaders at McKinsey. In fact, this "short-term" arrangement ended up lasting almost ten years. I was elected to partner and eventually senior partner, all while working on a part-time program. When my son was a bit older and no longer needed me at home as much, I went back to full time.

I showed the leaders at McKinsey that stepping sideways does not prevent a person from continuing to advance. Since my unconventional career move more than twenty years ago, this arrangement has turned into a standard career-track option for McKinsey employees. I'm proud of pioneering this flexible arrangement and helping the leaders after me find more balance in their work and personal life.

Christiana points out that she never would have been able to pioneer the part-time role if she hadn't accrued professional equity. She believed that McKinsey would want to keep her and would be willing to create a mutually satisfying solution. She'd reached that point of leverage after five years of working hard, doing well, and building internal support.

Later, she'd use that equity again when her son was in high school and needed extra attention. By then she was a senior partner and she decided she needed to be home and not travel during her son's high school years. Her firm's acquiescence wouldn't have happened had her colleagues not recognized that she'd be great in her administrative role and would later be returning to client work—which she did with continued success down the road.

These days, a lot of companies have flexible policies that allow people to work from home or have input in choosing their work schedules. Some companies are also willing to consider flexible career paths. A recent example at a senior level is Sarahjane Sacchetti, former CEO and now chief business officer for Cleo, which specializes in family benefits plans. Two and a half years after her stepfather was diagnosed with amyotrophic lateral sclerosis (ALS), a progressive neurogenerative disease, it became clear that the paid aides were no longer sufficient for his escalating care needs. She took a leave of absence from Cleo to become her stepfather's primary caregiver and to manage his affairs in his final months of life. When he died in December 2022, Sacchetti felt gratified that she'd made the choice to spend that precious time with him. It had led to an important decision—to step down as CEO and take a more limited role as chief business officer. This would allow her to spend more time with her widowed mother and her two young children. She explained her decision to *Fortune*'s Broadsheet as unusual—"We kind of go along straight lines in our careers"— but important.[4] The truth is, family caretaking demands can no longer be shoved under the rug. The pressures bearing down on women in the so-called sandwich generation—who are caught between the demands of caring for their children and their elderly parents—will continue to be felt and must be understood by firms that want to retain top talent at the executive level.

If you're with a company that has flexible options, be careful not to view these benefits as an entitlement. You need to be wise about availing yourself of this flexibility, carefully modulating what you do and don't take advantage of to ensure your work performance remains stellar. Companies expect high performers to demonstrate emotional maturity, prudence, and good judgment in using flexible arrangements so that work performance and team deliverables aren't compromised. Again, it's a question of taking a holistic view that accommodates your needs as well as the company's.

The good news is that being a stellar performer at work opens doors for you to earn more flexibility and leverage. By proving you can be counted on to exceed expectations, you gain chits that can be cashed in. When managers don't have a reason to question your ability to do your job well, it's a lot easier to ask for what you need—and get it with no strings attached.

Just keep in mind that the equity bank account isn't a given. You need to invest in maintaining a positive balance, as we've said earlier. This happens through consistent performance, a focus on growth and development, and good judgment.

Lose the Guilt

If you're a high-achieving person, you care deeply about excelling at everything you do. This drive can help you thrive, but it can also produce unrealistic expectations about what success looks like—especially when it comes to balancing your career with all the other aspects of life.

To live in a 360-degree way, you need to lose the guilt and think more about what you need to do for yourself.

To start, realize how often your feelings of guilt are about not measuring up to your own self-imposed standards. For example, if your vision of being perfect means that you bake from scratch, sew your kids' Halloween costumes, train for a triathlon, and visit your elderly relatives weekly, you're forcing yourself into a difficult position. While some other parents might be this involved, it's not the only way to raise a family.

On the flip side, you shouldn't feel guilty about not being able to dedicate every waking hour to your job. Of course, you want to surpass expectations, but you might need to check yourself if work is beginning to encroach on other aspects of your life that you regard as non-negotiable.

Grace

In what now feels like a former life, I once had a job where leaders were expected to reply to emails and texts within two hours—even on weekends or evenings. The expectation was part of the company culture and was meant to ensure that employees were responsive and nothing got bottlenecked. I took that working norm seriously. So seriously that the CEO once told me I was the most responsive person in the entire company. I see now that this wasn't a good thing—and it shouldn't have been a compliment, although she meant it as one. Instead, it was a sign that I had let my professional life overtake my personal time.

I've always had a passion and intensity for my job, viewing it as a personal imperative that I do as much as I possibly can for my company. In hindsight, I could have easily dialed it back and still been judged a high performer. In the latter years of my career, I developed a much healthier relationship with work. I remained 100 percent committed to top performance and set boundaries ensuring room for my personal life.

You might not realize how consumed you've gotten with work until you transition from being a young single person to being responsible for family. When this happens, you need to find a new rhythm that better balances your work and personal life. This is true whether you have a new baby, your parents are aging and need more help, or your partner becomes sick. The reality is when you have this kind of responsibility, you need to invite additional support into your life.

Keep in mind that if you feel like you aren't showing up for the people who matter most, it can damage your ability to be great at your job. Think about it: If you're worrying about your child who's sick, can you really be fully present in your client meetings? No matter how dedicated you are to your job, nothing will ever top the well-being of your family, and you shouldn't feel guilty about that. That said, you're paid to do a job, and the company should expect you to deliver on those commitments. Be clear on the trade-offs and expectations and get support to balance those moments.

Every CEO we've ever worked with has had to leave at some point for a family obligation. This is a good thing to keep in mind, especially if you're in a profession where employees often work ten-plus hours a day. This kind of grueling schedule is rarely sustainable in the long term, not just because you will burn out, but because family commitments are another part of you. If you're always at work and don't flex for those important moments in your personal life, you may miss out on the times that, in retrospect, mattered most to you. As the saying goes, "There are no do-overs in life."

Christiana

When my son was young, I agreed to host a neighborhood holiday cookie decorating party at my home on a Friday afternoon. Not only was it important to my son that we host, I *wanted* to do it—I traveled often, so I didn't get a lot of chances to socialize with my neighbors. I knew it wouldn't be possible for me to attend every gathering, but I wanted to be there for the ones that mattered most.

When it came time to leave the office, of course a small crisis came up that needed to be addressed. I'll be honest, I thought for a minute about saying I was leaving for a doctor's appointment, but you know what? My team thought it was awesome when I said I needed to go host a neighborhood party, and they rallied to ensure the small crisis was resolved without me. As a manager, I knew it was my responsibility to set an example for my consulting teams that it was okay to prioritize important obligations, and my stepping away gave some of the team members a chance to handle an issue on their own. This situation really helped set the tone for our local office's culture. Associates began to feel much more comfortable speaking up when they had personal commitments they needed to handle during work hours.

Managing a 360-Degree Life

Think of your 360-degree life as an intentionality wheel. Sometimes you choose "show up at your kids' events," sometimes you choose "schedule a checkup," sometimes you choose "get in an afternoon run"—and so on. The difference with the 360-degree life approach is that you are being intentional about what lands at the top, not leaving that to other people or circumstances. There are countless individual situations, but they tend to fall into familiar categories. Many of the circumstances you face might be different from those we encountered when we were coming up in our careers. However, the patterns seem evergreen and span generations. If you recognize those patterns, you can reach for tools that will help you through it.

No matter how you spin the 360-degree wheel, you can learn from the following seven practical strategies.

1. **Create your own give-and-take.** Sometimes the stress of a 360-degree life is a matter of time conflicts that demand a strategic response. Even if you're able to set up a custom schedule that allows you to take time off during the normal workday, it's important to realize that the job pace and intensity don't slow down when you're gone. It's nice for employers to acknowledge the concessions you need, but it's up to you to figure out how to make the adaptations. Work you're paid to do still needs to get done. You can ask for leeway on deadlines, but you still need to do the work. You need to be very mindful about how you spend your time so that you're as effective as possible when you return.

2. **Be intentional and balanced in asking for personal exceptions.** Whenever you step outside the conventional norms of your workplace, it can be uncomfortable. Many people worry that asking for a personal accommodation is going to put limits on their career, so they don't do it. It shouldn't be that way. Instead of assuming it's impossible, come up with a plan for making it work for both the company and you. It's not one-sided. You won't get what you need without asking for it, and you might just be surprised that your employer is more than willing to accommodate.

   Again, when you've built up credibility through your performance and feel confident you can keep up with your job responsibilities, you're well positioned to have better balance in your life overall. Can you go in early so you can leave early for a period of time? Do you need to scale back to a part-time arrangement for a year? Sometimes these kinds of adjustments can seem impossible if no one else at your organization is attempting them, but don't let that deter you. Be honest with yourself about what you need and what it takes to do your job. Then share your proposal with your company while building confidence that you will continue to produce quality work.

The key is intentionality and clarity on how the company can trust that your high job performance will continue. Remember, your life and your career exist within a relationship with the company.

3. **Ask for support.** This is about empowerment. Some people will assume that their employers, their teams, or their bosses won't be willing to meet them halfway with something they need, so they don't ask for it. We talked about this with salary negotiations, and it's the same here. Don't negotiate with yourself. Ask for what you need.

Coming up with a solution that both you and your employer feel good about could take some negotiating. You might not get everything you ask for, and that's okay. Instead of getting upset that you need to pull back on your requests, figure out what's most important to you—and your family. When you identify those "essentials," you can hold on to them and let go of the rest.

Keep being strategic. For example, it may be easier to get what you want if it's not permanent. You know, "I need this flex for this period of time." Or "How about a trial period where we agree to evaluate at the end of six months?" If things are working well for you and the company, you can always come back and talk about extending. Provide opportunities to get to yes.

4. **Realize that self-care isn't selfish.** To underscore: LeanIn and McKinsey's Women in the Workplace report, which surveyed 423 organizations and 65,000 employees, revealed that 42 percent of women said they often or almost always feel burned out. That was up from 32 percent the year before, and 7 percentage points higher than their male peers.[5]

    When you take proper care of yourself, you're able to help others and bring your best self to work. You should view your career as a long game; it's especially important to get into a solid routine where you prioritize your physical and mental well-being.

    If you don't take care of your body, it will catch up to you later in life. You want to keep living a vibrant, active life when you hit your fifties and sixties and beyond, so it's smart to focus on your health now. Go to the doctor and dentist regularly, eat healthfully, and get as much sleep as you possibly can. Even if you're beyond busy, figure out how to exercise on a regular basis. Maybe that means taking some less important calls while you're out walking or doing a twenty-minute YouTube workout in your hotel room before your meetings. Such small acts of self-care might seem trivial, but in the grand scheme of things, they go a long way to compensate for the toll that a fast-paced, high-intensity career can take on your body. (Among the most self-sabotaging actions: sitting in front of a computer all day without getting up regularly and moving around, getting up early and staying up late, powering through colds, traveling constantly.)

Pay attention to how you're feeling mentally. Taking a short break to meditate and focus on breathing has been shown to lower stress and calm the nervous system. Schedule and keep your regular health checkups and prioritize those appointments. Think at least twice before canceling vacations or working every weekend. It's easy to let self-care habits slide, especially when life becomes overwhelming, but that's when you need to take care of yourself the most.

Grace

When I was thirty-nine, I was crushing it at my job, finding joy at home with my kids, and relishing my life as a very healthy woman. One day, I found out I had a tumor in my stomach. My doctors were very concerned and told me that it could either be a specific benign non-recurring type of tumor or an alternative type that could mean death in six months. They would need to do surgery either way to find out, and the operation presented a one-in-300 chance of dying on the table, since the tumor was close to my aorta.

I thought about how my ex-husband would need to raise our kids. At the time, they were only twelve and nine years old, and they'd need many years of loving care and direction. It was a surreal time, especially for someone in their late thirties. I relied heavily on prayers and trust in God during this very difficult period.

Luckily the surgery went well, and the tumor turned out to be benign. I was in the ICU for seven days, and whether it was the medication playing tricks with my perception or a true visitation, I recall seeing an angel at the foot of my bed during one of my nights there. It gave me peace and reassurance. Somewhere in the middle of that hospital stay, my boss called me to touch base. Our company was going through a restructuring, and apparently, she thought it must have been on my mind. After she inquired about my health, she said, "Don't worry. You have a spot." In that moment, I was struck by the fact that I wasn't at all concerned about whether I'd still have a job at the company after it was restructured. I had my life, and my kids had a loving parent who would continue to be there for them; that was all that mattered. (I also knew I was very good at my job and would bounce back easily.)

It was a poignant reminder of how unimportant work is compared with health. I never forgot this lesson. After my surgery, I went back to work with a fresh perspective. To this day, I prioritize my doctor visits and health checkups. I've never lost my passion for my work, and I've gained a newfound appreciation for taking care of myself.

You know what happens when you forget to charge your cell phone. It's no different with your personal energy management. You need to recharge. When you take proper care of yourself, you're able to help others and bring your best self to work. In the long journey of your career, it's especially important to get into a solid routine where you prioritize your health.

5. **Ramp up your personal support system.** Putting in place the support you need can take many forms: a meal delivery service

such as DoorDash, a laundry service, a regular babysitter, a housekeeper, or a teenage neighbor to cut your lawn or run errands. Sure, when you're at the bottom of the career ladder, a support system will feel like a luxury you can't afford (that's why parents were invented). In time, though, you'll climb the ladder's rungs, and sooner than you think it'll make sense to reach out for help with life's routine tasks.

Don't feel guilty for paying someone else to take nonwork to-dos off your plate, even when affording it is still a stretch. It's not a splurge; it's a strategy. When you can scale back on obligations that conflict with your work schedule, as well as tasks that could be done by someone else, you free up your time to thrive both at work and at home. In hindsight, we realized that the money we spent getting sustainable support at home, especially when our kids were young, was one of the key investments propelling us to success.

6. **Adapt with the times.** As both your kids and your parents get older, your needs also evolve. The perfect situation today might not work for you in a year, and that's okay. Flex arrangements can be temporary. In fact, it's best to think of them as temporary from the beginning. It can give you comfort if you're going through a difficult patch, and it can help your company be more open to offering concessions.

7. **Create rituals and special moments to stay connected.** To manage the spillover effect in our lives and stay connected with loved ones, we both learned to create special rituals or moments. For instance, Grace would take her son out to get pancakes in the morning on occasional school days.

Christiana would always do a wake-up and a good-night call to her son when she was traveling for work, regardless of what time zone she was in or what time of day it was for her. Other effective rituals could be coffee with your partner at the start of each day, or a weekly lunch date outside the office to ensure you step away from your desk. Whatever it is, the idea is to schedule and value these moments as much as any meeting or work event.

When in Doubt, Go Back to Your Cardinal Direction

Throughout your career, the challenges will ebb and flow. Sometimes you'll encounter significant disruptions that will throw you off-balance. When that happens, it helps to remember that the situation is temporary and you can get through it. The best way to do this is to go back to your Cardinal Direction. Think about what's most important to you in the long term. What's worth fighting for? What *aren't* you willing to put up with? And what could make your situation better? Asking those questions will help you find clarity during the most trying times.

And remember *why* you're doing it—not just for job security but because your career counts. You've heard the saying "It's the journey, not the destination." Our point is that it's the journey *and* the destination. You can find joy in meeting the challenges of your career as it's happening, and joy in looking back at what you've been through. That's the payoff of Career Forward.

Living a 360-degree life offers a different perspective than the tired old theme of work/life balance. It allows you to embrace your life in all its aspects. If you can master that approach, you'll no longer think of the stress of balancing the different parts of your life as an unrelenting chore. Over time you'll begin to look at your menu of options with new eyes, intentionally choosing where to place your focus. The wheel won't spin out of your control. You'll have it firmly in hand.

Grace

Living a 360-degree life served me well. At the heart of it were an ability to be clear on what to prioritize and managing the timing of decisions. I also maintained a deep appreciation for the joy of my work and the joy of my family.

When my daughter entered high school, I was committed to giving her the stability and oversight she needed during those critical years. At the same time, the employment market was hot and my career equity positioned me to be recruited for chief procurement officer positions, which typically required relocating from our home in Chicago.

I decided that it would be disruptive to my daughter to move her at this critical life stage, so I intentionally decided to stay at my current company and looked for a local CPO role as my next career move knowing it might take a bit longer to achieve.

I had a Career Forward mindset and knew that a CPO role was the natural next step and within my grasp. I found a way to keep my career progression going by choosing to take only local opportunities that also offered the right career growth potential. When the United Airlines CPO job materialized, it gave me valuable experience in leading the procurement function and in being part of a senior leadership team that transformed the company, not least by executing a corporate merger. These experiences ended up being a springboard for me to take one of the largest CPO roles in the market on the East Coast a few years later. My choice to stay in Chicago for those few extra years became a win-win. It was good for my daughter, and because I was strategic, it was good for my career.

KEY TAKEAWAYS

- Don't buy into the fixed work-life trade-off mindset.

- Leverage your professional equity to make work "work" for you.

- Get the best support you can afford—the investment will pay off.

- Lose the guilt. You can't have a successful long-term career without taking care of yourself.

9

Lucky Like a Duck

Rarely are opportunities presented to you in a perfect way. In a nice little box with a yellow bow on top. "Here, open it, it's perfect. You'll love it." Opportunities—the good ones—are messy, confusing, and hard to recognize. They're risky. They challenge you.

—Susan Wojcicki, CEO, YouTube

When a duck glides over water, it looks calm, graceful, and effortless. But we don't see what's happening under the surface—that constant movement of the duck's feet, even when it's floating in place. When it comes to professional success, we might have a lot to learn from ducks.

Sometimes it seems as if certain people glide through life, enjoying one good fortune after another. They make it look so easy that others even credit their success to luck. (*That opportunity fell into her lap . . . she was in the right place at the right time.*) We don't always see the hard work and intentionality that often go into making success look easy. In fact, we've learned that you can do a lot to create your own professional luck through a combination of recognition, responsiveness, and readiness—and that notion can be very empowering. A young woman Christiana mentors recently mentioned that while some people might have more opportunities, the idea of making her own luck gave her a greater sense of control over her life. Once she adopted this mindset, she was able to recognize ways she'd created her own luck over the years. As she shared, "Some people may come with more cards on the table, but there are always ways to take control of your life and identify opportunities."

Create the Conditions to Excel

As an executive at PepsiCo, Grace was presented with the opportunity to go to the World Economic Forum (WEF) in Davos, Switzerland, which is considered one of the world's premier business leadership conferences. The WEF brings together top business leaders, government leaders, academics, economists, and other experts and influencers in a variety of industries to discuss key global issues. The event in Davos is five days long with many sessions for attendees.

When a colleague mentioned to her how lucky she was to be selected multiple times for such an enviable trip, Grace assured her that luck had nothing to do with it. Although she appreciated the career benefit that regularly attending the event could provide, she knew that winning the opportunity had involved a tremendous amount of work.

She always came prepared for the extensive engagement and learning opportunities, and before selecting which forums to attend, she carefully researched the topics and the individuals involved. She considered what gain could accrue to the company's business. And in the forums she chose, she sought broader exposure to world issues and insight on the evolution of emerging technologies. Davos also brought significant opportunities for networking, so she made a point to engage in one-on-one meetings with key world leaders. After each full day of sessions, dinners, and networking, she went back to her room and spent the next hour reflecting and writing a summary of what she'd learned. She then took the time to share that takeaway with the PepsiCo executive team to make sure her knowledge was transferred.

The hard work and strategy paid off. Grace was invited to attend Davos multiple times during her career at PepsiCo. It might seem as if leaders get lucky when they're selected for this kind of role, but casual observers often don't see the work individuals put in behind the scenes to be presented with such opportunities, and how these take-the-initiative types leverage them into something bigger.

Recognition: Spotting Opportunity When It Knocks

Although you can't always control the opportunities that come your way, you can control your perspective. To prime yourself for luck, you need to keep your eyes peeled. You know those special projects that seem a little too far outside of your comfort zone? Or the events that would require you to miss something else you want to do? Think about what might happen if you didn't automatically say no to getting involved. You could very well find yourself on a stepping-stone to something much more exciting. Maybe you'd learn a new skill that could bring an unexpected chance to collaborate on an exciting project, or perhaps you'd meet someone who'd prove to be influential months down the road. There have been countless times in our careers when we've looked back and pinpointed a key moment that had an oversize impact.

Christiana

Six weeks after I gave birth to my son, I got a call from one of the partners at my consulting firm asking if I'd help with a retail client proposal. It would involve structuring the proposal, being involved in proposal meetings, and forming a relationship with the key client executive—all of which would take time away from home and my new baby. Initially, I thought of many reasons to say no: I'd never consulted in the retail industry, none of my work clothes fit yet, my baby was feeding every three hours, and on top of that, I was completely sleep-deprived. I almost told the partner I couldn't help and that I'd be back in the office in six more weeks, as planned.

But when I thought more about the opportunity, I realized something important—the client was local. That was rare in my line of work. I was used to traveling across the country on a weekly basis to be on-site with clients, which was a lot less attractive for a new mom. If I was able to get an assignment with a client who was based in town, I knew it would dramatically smooth my transition back to the office after my maternity leave ended.

So I decided to say yes to the opportunity. I fastened my too-tight skirt with a rubber band, shook off the post-baby brain fog, and showed up to all the meetings. The client ultimately signed on with our firm, and I was given the manager role for the project—which turned into three full years with the same client, and a lot less travel while my child was young.

When colleagues heard about my getting this plum opportunity, they'd often say something like "Wow, you really lucked out!" In a way they were right—it was serendipity that the potential client reached out when they did—but that wasn't all it took for me to "be lucky." I'd developed a strong working relationship over several years with the partner who brought me in, and when opportunity knocked, I recognized it and made a strategic decision that ultimately shaped the future of my career. Instead of selecting the option that was easier in the short term, I thought about the long-term potential. Nothing would have come of serendipity if I hadn't recognized that a door was opening for me.

It's important to note that while we're major advocates for saying yes to new experiences and taking on opportunities beyond your core responsibilities, we're *not* advising you to say yes to everything that comes your way. Be thoughtful, strategic, and invest your time where you believe it will have a high return. In effect, practice the growth stock mindset we shared earlier.

Here are a few questions you should ask yourself if a potentially meaningful professional opportunity surfaces: Will the opportunity help you . . .

- Make new connections or relationships?
- Sharpen a priority skill set?
- Boost your reputation—e.g., for learning agility or a can-do attitude?
- Drive notable business impact?
- Differentiate you from your peers (in either capacity or breadth)?

All of these are solid signs that professional opportunity is knocking on your door—all you need to do is let it in. You never know what little thing could end up changing your life—even decades later. Make sure you pay attention and see opportunity for what it truly is. Sometimes things that seemed like happenstance end up being pivotal for years to come.

Responsiveness: Making the Most of an Opportunity

Have you ever wondered how two people can be presented with the exact same opportunity, but end up with entirely different outcomes? We believe a lot of it is based on how they respond. Just like a choose-your-own-adventure story, there will undoubtably be times when you have the power to turn seemingly mundane experiences into opportunities to build professional equity. You'll derive greater benefits just by leaning into an experience and proactively trying to get the most out of it. When you engage in an opportunity or new assignment, be enthusiastic, proactive, and optimistic. When it comes to performance, you want to double down and make sure you don't waste your chance.

Readiness: Creating Your Own Luck

Now that you know what opportunity looks like and how to make the most of it, it's time to make the "luck" come to you. This is the difference between waiting for someone to pass you the ball and going after it yourself. We always recommend taking the initiative, rather than standing back, because it gives you greater control and you're much more likely to make things happen quickly.

The Roman philosopher Seneca once famously observed, "Luck is what happens when preparation meets opportunity." Preparation creates the conditions to be lucky, and we think it's a great skill to build over the course of your career. Pamela Neferkará, Christiana's colleague from Nike who handled marketing there, has done this particularly well. After spending nearly two decades in the sports industry, she was looking for an opportunity to flex her skills in a different industry. She began thinking about pursuing a board position as a way of achieving these goals.

Pamela chose to pursue a board position at this stage of her career for two reasons. She told us: "First, I felt that it was a natural progression to continue to operate at a strategic leadership level. And I knew that I could bring to bear a lot of my skills and experiences. And second, I'm a real believer that diversity comes from the top down, and in a company, the board is the absolute top. A wider range of voices around the table influences how companies operate. So I thought it was important to raise my hand and say, 'Yes, I want a seat at the table.'"

Pamela was aware of the odds, since only 4 percent of board directors are black women.[1] So she took steps over several years to make her own opportunity. To start, she developed a list of criteria to help her assess opportunities. She wanted to join a mission-driven company she could relate to. The company needed to be located somewhere she could travel to relatively easily for meetings. Having these and other criteria prepared her to weigh opportunities and choose the best fit.

Next, Pamela set herself up to be qualified to take on a board role. Realizing that her lack of experience could be an impediment, she joined the board of trustees at the middle school her son had attended. She also signed up for a highly regarded board preparedness class tailored specifically to women looking for their first board role. This allowed Pamela to learn a great deal about how boards operate and positioned her well to be a strong candidate.

Pamela acknowledges, however, that it wasn't just her personal preparation that set her up to succeed. Her timing was fortuitous—i.e., opportunity knocked and she was ready for it. As Pamela notes, "In all candor, I believe the opportunity presented itself because of the civil unrest in the United States in 2020, which created a real reckoning for all companies to think differently about diversity in much more than just a performative way," she said. "I got my first board role because there was a greater call for diversity in the boardroom. A lot of organizations began to spring up that were essentially creating databases of female board-ready candidates, including one I was introduced to in Silicon Valley. And honestly, within the first four weeks of their having my board bio, I got a phone call, and that's how I landed my first board role."

We recognize that Pamela's specific goal (joining a board) is one you may not target until later in your career, but her strategic approach is something you can use early and often. As you consider how to create your own opportunities, here are a few strategies to guide you:

Give yourself every chance. Luck happens to those who look for it and are ready to take full advantage. Think of ways you can be at the right place at the right time. Telegraph openness in your professional dealings. And don't forget to directly ask for advancement opportunities. Here's an example of a script for opening that dialogue—in this case asking to move from being an individual contributor to being a manager and expanding your scope of responsibilities.

I'd like to talk to you about my role within our company and the next opportunities for development. I enjoy working here and have really appreciated being able to develop in my current position. I believe I am ready now to increase my contribution and further my development with the expansion of my role into that of a team manager. I'd like to get your support to make that move.

As we've discussed in my past reviews, I've been building field expertise and collaboration and leadership skills.

I am confident that moving to manage others now would unleash my and the team's full potential and have a positive impact on the company.

Do you support this next step for me? If so, what do you think are the best next steps and timing to proceed?

Develop authentic sponsor relationships. Sabrina Simmons, the former Gap CFO with whom we both worked on the Williams-Sonoma board, told us that she dislikes what she calls contrived networking and contrived mentoring. Networking and mentoring work only when they're built on authentic relationships. We agree with this perspective. Sabrina tells people: "Go work with leaders you admire—you'll learn from them." She highlights the value of listening, watching, and learning from leaders. She thinks listening and watching are underrated skills. She was at Gap at a moment when there was a host of incredible women at the brand president level whom she could work with and learn from. They took responsibility for supporting her career development. She learned from them and made it a point to do the same for the women coming up behind her.

Christiana

As a young manager, I remember the time I had to give a presentation to an important senior client. I worked hard on the material, and I was pleased that it seemed to be well received by the group. After the session, we took a break and I headed to the ladies' room. While I was washing my hands, a woman senior partner who had been in the meeting came in and congratulated me for doing a good job. Then she told me a few things that I could do even better next time. Her immediate feedback was so helpful, since the experience was fresh in my mind.

At that moment, it struck me that this was the kind of timely feedback my male colleagues had probably been getting after presentations for years. I was used to being the only woman in the meeting room, and thus the only woman in the ladies' restroom. But the rest of my colleagues were always chatting on their way to and from the men's room before and after meetings.

Any kind of informal interactions with senior leaders can be helpful, especially when a person is trying to learn the ropes of a new position or craft an emerging skill set. I realized that perhaps I'd been missing out on that, just because of the lack of female leaders above me. I told myself that I wanted to become the person who'd proactively help the women climbing up the career ladder behind me.

Think five moves ahead. Predicting a potential domino effect can be difficult, but that's often the best way to prioritize and anticipate potential. As an example, if a teamwork initiative would enable you to form a relationship with someone who works directly in a part of the company you're interested in, that could end up helping you network for opportunities later.

Align with the zeitgeist. In every company, there are hot topics that key leaders want to focus on. If you hear an EVP say, "We need people to work on addressing X," that's a good sign that the work will be valued within the organization. Hot topics typically correlate with high-impact opportunities for the business.

Go after the difficult work. When work initiatives are clearly going to be challenging, a lot of people feel intimidated. If you volunteer to take on that kind of work, you can put your learning into overdrive. Your willingness to take the lead will also boost your reputation in a meaningful way. This can differentiate you as someone who can fill broader roles in the future.

Believe in yourself. Get comfortable raising your hand to take on more or lean into an experience that you may not know as well as you would like but trust you will learn and figure out. Yes, there's a risk to taking on additional responsibilities, especially when you're not totally sure what they entail. But if you commit to doing your best, the odds of your being successful are certainly in your favor. Demonstrating your self-assuredness will also help you along the way. When you project confidence in yourself, it boosts others' confidence in you, which continues to open more doors of opportunity.

As you blaze a career path, keep putting in the work to create the right conditions for being lucky. Sometimes the perfect project or job will fall right into your lap, but most of the time you'll need to maneuver yourself into the right position using a combination of hard work and savvy strategy.

Christiana

To this day I remember an incident early in my career when I was an associate at Merrill. It was my first serious job, my second year out of college. I was working with an intern, a college student who was one of those "shiny pennies" we've talked about. She wanted to show up only when she could gain an advantage.

She and I were doing all the grunt work on a big presentation, and the intern was bummed because our boss had made it clear that we wouldn't be invited into the room for the meeting. No junior people were allowed. She was grumbling about it, and suddenly someone poked their head out of the boardroom and said there was a mistake on page whatever. I flipped through the report, and sure enough, there was the error, which had been made by me and the intern.

We had to rush to fix it and reprint the page and take it into the meeting so everyone could replace the page in their copies. As we were running them off the printer, the intern said, "I'm not taking them in." She didn't want to be the face of the mistake. Well, neither did I. I hated the idea of walking into the meeting under those circumstances. She was the intern, so it was clearly her job, but she wouldn't do it. So I said I would. I was the senior person, so it was ultimately my responsibility.

I walked in with the stack of corrected pages, and the room was filled with all the top executives at Merrill. I went over to hand the papers to my boss, who was sitting next to the treasurer. And the treasurer said, "Oh, Christiana, why don't you sit down." I stayed for the entire meeting. I realized that had I not brought in the pages, I never would have had the opportunity. I made my own luck that day by taking responsibility.

The intern was livid that she'd missed the chance to be in the meeting, but I also learned something. People in the meeting didn't think twice about replacing the page. It wasn't the end of the world. It happened all the time. So the high anxiety had been misplaced.

A final tip: When you start looking for "luck," you will see that there are opportunities everywhere. It's like discovering a new color on the spectrum that you can't unsee. With your eye trained to spot luck every day, you'll be amazed at the opportunities you'll find.

KEY TAKEAWAYS

- Opportunities are everywhere. The trick is to spot them and step up.

- You can create your own professional luck through a combination of recognition, responsiveness, and readiness.

- Think ahead: What opportunities can you create for the future by saying yes now?

10

Facing the Forks in the Road

When you come to a fork in the road, be still, and see with your mind's eye. There you find the clarity you seek.

—Michelle Cruz-Rosado, author and empowerment expert

Our friend Miriam Ort has an intriguing story of her encounter with a particularly dramatic fork in the road. Miriam is the chief human resources officer at C&S Wholesale Grocers and coauthor of the bestselling book *One Page Talent Management: Eliminating Complexity, Adding Value*.[1] She worked incredibly hard to get where she is today, and she might not have gotten there without taking an unexpected detour.

At a midpoint in her career, Miriam was offered an opportunity to move to Europe to take an expat assignment. While she was excited about the role and confident it was the right career move, it wasn't the right time for her husband to move. They both acknowledged this and discussed what could be done about the situation.

"We made the decision that I would move, and he would remain in the United States," said Miriam. "While I knew that this was an unconventional approach, I was surprised at how uncomfortable the decision made people, including my own leadership. I had leaders in the company pulling me aside to encourage me to pass—either assuming I wouldn't truly relocate and would thus not do justice to the job, or worried that I was making a personal 'sacrifice' that went too far."

Ultimately, Miriam took the role and made the move. She says it was one of the best experiences not only of her career but of her whole life. She doesn't sugarcoat the personal trade-offs involved, but she says she was always 100 percent comfortable with them because she made the decision in line with her personal priorities.

"Passing on that role would have been one of the biggest mistakes of my career," she said. "While the many people advising me to take a pass were wrong, they had good intentions. Ultimately, when it comes to these tough decisions and trade-offs, you usually already know the answer. The trick is to not let conventional thinking get in the way of what you know, in your heart, is most important to you."

Like Miriam, you might make choices that cause some people you know to feel uncomfortable. This can happen in countless situations, such as switching industries or job functions, making a lateral move, taking a job at a smaller company or start-up, accepting a job that has lower compensation, or even staying in a role that isn't your dream job. There are myriad factors to consider—both professional and personal—and the trade-offs you're willing to make are unique to you.

Should You Stay or Should You Go?

Sometimes fear of the unknown makes it seem easier and safer to stay put even when you'd prefer to make a change. Inertia can also be a powerful force, and a key reason many people continue in the same role at the same company, doing the same tasks for far too long. But keeping your head down and cruising along without questioning where you're going is akin to being asleep at the wheel, and it's definitely not a Career Forward posture. If you aren't progressing in your career, it's a sign that you may be at a very common fork in the road in your professional journey, asking, "Should I stay or should I go?"

We want to be clear about what career advancement is really about, since it isn't just measured by money or titles. If you're learning, growing, and making an impact at your organization in new ways, you certainly aren't stagnant. The experiences you're having are valuable for crafting your skills and ability to contribute, and you're also building your reputation and resume.

However, if you're staying in a position because of inertia, and you're no longer growing or stretching yourself, something needs to change. Otherwise, you're "burning daylight," which you'll never get back again. When this happens, you have only two options: create momentum at your current job or start looking elsewhere.

Knowing when to leave a job can be tricky, especially since companies are often eager to paint a rosy picture when it comes to future opportunities. You can chalk this up to being optimistic or not wanting to lose talent. Sometimes it does take time for the right opportunity to come around at an organization—for instance, if the position above you needs to be vacated for you to be promoted. But if you've been in a holding pattern and are losing valuable career time as you wait, it's time to consider a move.

It's kind of like being in a relationship where your partner keeps saying they're going to take you home to meet their family, but the holidays pass season after season and you're still waiting for an invitation. You might decide to apply pressure to get what you want, and might even issue an ultimatum. If you do, you might get what you want in the short term, but being in this situation in the first place is usually a sign of an underlying issue. You want your partner to be excited about taking your relationship to the next level without being pressured into it. The same is true for your employer. If you're consistently a top performer, you should not find yourself in a place where you need to ring the company's doorbell to force a discussion on progression. We encourage you to avoid using ultimatums. Instead, simply be candid with the company about your capabilities and interests in expanding your role. However, if that does not result in satisfactory progress, you should remember that you have options. High performers and Career Forward–minded people know they can cultivate new opportunities.

Christiana

When I was up for senior partner, I got an offer out of the blue to take a very senior role at a major dot-com. I found myself at an unexpected fork in the road. For years, I'd had my sights set on advancing at McKinsey and ultimately making senior partner, but I had no way of knowing for sure if or when it was going to happen. I'd always performed well, but there were many talented people vying for limited spots. I was eager to continue advancing my career—whether at my current job or another—so I was torn about what to do.

I decided to be honest with leaders at McKinsey and tell them I was considering this unexpected offer, just so they'd know where my head was at. I was careful about how I broached the conversation, as I didn't want them to think I was trying to give them an ultimatum. I had the feeling that people wouldn't respond positively to anything that smacked of an ultimatum, and it could easily backfire—either immediately or down the road.

I took time to evaluate the dot-com opportunity, meet the investors behind the business, and understand what the role would involve. Ultimately, I decided not to accept the job. My gut told me that my options were still richer at McKinsey, and it was reassuring to know that if things didn't work out at the firm, I'd likely be able to find attractive external options. I made my choice clear to McKinsey well before the elections for senior partner took place, which signaled to leadership that I wasn't trying to force their hand, and shortly afterward I was elected senior partner.

Sometime after that, I was chatting with a leader who was on the elections committee, and I mentioned that I was intentional about not trying to use the dot-com job offer as leverage to get promoted. He confirmed that I'd made the right choice and said it signaled to the other leaders that I wasn't trying to hold them over a barrel, but rather genuinely trying to make a difficult and important choice.

We can't stress enough how delicate the situation can be when you're considering whether to stay at your company or pursue work elsewhere. It's a risky and even foolish negotiating move to try to pit companies against each other in order to secure a better offer. Trust us, companies don't want to take part in that kind of bidding war. Even if in the short term you get the job or compensation you want, there's a good chance you'll damage your reputation at both companies.

To be clear, there *is* a right way to negotiate with your current company. Sometimes people who are considering outside offers forget to consider what it would take for them to stay where they are. If you submit your resignation, there's a good chance your boss or HR head will ask you how the company could persuade you *not* to go. Don't make up your mind to leave if you haven't already considered whether certain changes would convince you to stay. Give your company the courtesy and benefit of directly understanding your expectations and needs before you jump into a new pond. As a first step, consider the five questions you should ask before beginning a job search:

1) What are the gaps in my current role, and why are they important to me for career advancement?

2) Am I more likely to get to my next career goal by applying for a new position at my current company or by changing companies?

3) What are the main capabilities I have that could be better leveraged? How would my desire to elevate my contributions have greater value in a new job?

4) Would a new company and/or new job provide me with a runway to the next two or three advancement steps in the company?

5) Do I have people in my network who can help connect me to external opportunities? If not, what steps should I take first, before starting a search?

This gets even more complex when family and financial obligations are factored in. Sometimes you can put yourself and your career first, but other times, you have to prioritize elsewhere.

STEP-up to the Moment

If life was totally predictable, it would be boring. Not knowing exactly how things will shape up keeps us on our toes. We've talked about how you can create professional opportunities for yourself, but for better or worse, important career choices can also arise unexpectedly. With a Career Forward mentality, you'll be prepared for a fork in the road and have at least some directional principles you can apply when you stand between two choices. It would be amazing to have a crystal ball to reveal the future and help you choose the right path, but that's not how life (or a career journey) works. Instead of a crystal ball, what we can give you is a framework for making those pivotal career decisions. We call it STEP-up, which is an acronym for sequenced actions you should take:

S – Stop and breathe

T – Think through the trade-offs

E – Evaluate and decide

P – Put the pedal down

Stop and breathe.

When you face a choice about the direction you want to head in your career, it's a big moment. Take a breath—literally. Go for a walk, sit on a bench by the water, take a yoga class, make a list—whatever will open your mind. You may be feeling the pressure to make a decision quickly, but you deserve the time to reflect and reconnect with your goals.

This step is about centering yourself and opening yourself to think clearly. You're about to make a major decision, and it demands a clear, calm perspective. Relax and focus on becoming present to what's in front of you.

Think through the trade-offs.

Even when you know where you want to go in your career, you'll likely be faced with tough decisions from time to time. This is especially true when it comes to balancing trade-offs, which are a difficult but inevitable part of professional life.

Every choice you make involves a trade-off. Most opportunities aren't 100 percent perfect, so you need to have a clear understanding of what matters the most to you.

As we described above, you might have to consider making adjustments to your family life, where you live, or your preferred work environment. If the conditions are not ideal, try to negotiate around the issues. Maybe you'll decide, as Miriam Ort did, that the opportunity is worth a temporary family disruption. Maybe you can justify pushing the envelope for a couple of years if it earns a crucial promotion. It all comes down to where the opportunity sits in the context of your broader goals and interests.

Evaluate and decide.

A fork in the road is a choice between one path and another. Now is the time to get out your assessment toolbox to help you evaluate your choice. Revisit what's important to you in your career, with the Career Forward journey in mind. Does this opportunity align with your overall purpose? In what ways can you see it moving you down the road?

Also, what else is out there? Broaden your view of the marketplace beyond the opportunity you're considering. Whenever we're asked to give guidance to people who are considering an offer, particularly one that is unexpected, we suggest they look around a bit before they take it. Tap your network, including recruiters and contacts at other organizations, to find out what they're seeing. This unexpected offer could be an indication of a lot more opportunity out there for your experience and capabilities.

Put the pedal down.

When you approach difficult forks in the road, it's essential to remember that the best path for you is going to be different from the best path for someone else. There are many times in our careers when we make decisions that surprise our friends, families, and coworkers. People with our best interests at heart might encourage us to rethink our choices and make sure we're doing the right thing. If this happens to you, *don't* take it as a sign that you're about to make a mistake. Sometimes the path less traveled is the right choice, if it aligns with what you care about most and gets you closer to your ultimate goal.

Believe in yourself and the validity of your choices, and then tackle the new challenge with everything you've got.

. . . . .

A great example of the STEP-up approach is the process Grace used when she was considering a big move to join a consumer packaged goods company in a new city. It was a major opportunity, but she had to think it through.

Grace

I took time to breathe, to reflect. What did it mean for my career to take this huge job at such a phenomenal company? I spent a lot of time thinking it over, and I kept hearing this inner voice urging me to take a leap of faith. There was a lot of deep reflection. I had to evaluate the total implications of this offer. It was one of the largest chief procurement officer jobs available, hugely transformative, in an $80 billion company. It was a dream job. But there were trade-offs that had to be weighed, and conflicts between the personal and professional. It would mean a move from Chicago to New York when my son still had one more year of high school. I'd have to leave him behind with family and friends for that year and see him only part time. We were incredibly close, and it was a hard decision, although he was urging me to say yes. The job was going to require a tremendous amount of international travel. It would involve taking a decentralized procurement function and making it into a global function. That meant a massive amount of change management and complexity. I had to really think through how I'd balance the intense work time commitment and extensive international travel with the needs of my son at this critical high school life stage.

In the end I took the job, and it became one of the best experiences I had in my career. I was intellectually stimulated and inspired by the work and the relationships. My time there included room for a big and very full life, and my son thrived as well. During that last year of high school, he matured and became really independent, which set him up to be ready when he went away to college the next year. When I look back on that period, it was a growth experience for both of us.

Most people experience an ebb and flow in their career trajectory, especially as their priorities shift throughout their lives. Learn to treat those inflection points as an opportunity to reflect and reevaluate. Don't let them spook you. As you think about your career goals, keep your eyes peeled for forks in the road. Sometimes they're obvious, but sometimes they appear suddenly. More than anything, remember that the path to success isn't usually a straight line. No one knows you as well as you know yourself, so trust your gut.

KEY TAKEAWAYS

- Don't let fear of the unknown turn into inertia.

- When you're faced with a choice, use the STEP framework to evaluate the possibilities and choose a direction.

- Once you've made a choice, trust your gut and go for it.

11

Shaping Your Leadership Identity

*Having female leaders in positions of influence to serve
as role models is not only critical to the career advancement of women,
but stands to generate broader societal impacts on pay equity,
changing workplace policies in ways that benefit both men and
women, and attracting a more diverse workforce.*

— **Rockefeller Foundation, "Women in Leadership: Why It Matters"**

How many times when you were growing up did someone call you a leader or compliment you on your leadership? If you're like us, it may be hard to think of any.

Christiana remembers when her son was graduating from sixth grade. The principal proudly posed for a picture with him and told her, "This kid is a real leader. You need to make sure he lives up to his potential." Her son responded to the comment with great pride. He beamed and seemed to grow taller. Afterward, Christiana realized that no teacher had ever said anything like that about her to her mother when she was young, despite all the ways she'd excelled in school.

In fact, that kind of early encouragement has often been missing for girls, and it makes a difference in how they see themselves as leaders and how others see them—even though becoming an effective, authentic, inspiring leader is core to long-term career success. There are very few senior roles that don't have direct reports.

Throughout your career, be intentional about transitioning effectively into leadership roles. Learn how to navigate the complex social issue of getting promoted over your peers, how to assess your new team of reports, how to model the cultural changes you want to see at your organization, and how to develop your own unique leadership identity.

Why Leadership Is an Essential Skill

Many women in the early stages of their careers don't necessarily think of leadership skills as important to have. They can seem lofty and abstract. In fact, leadership is the foundation of a Career Forward path. It's something you can practice and prepare for even before you're in managerial positions. It's a skill that can be internalized for higher performance.

Companies look for leadership skills when they're promoting, and that's reason enough to take them seriously. But leadership skills are worth developing on their own merits. They help focus you on a vision, enable you to organize your strategic priorities, and make it possible for you to oversee effective collaboration.

As you advance in your role, your job requirements become increasingly complex, as do your leadership responsibilities. Chances are, you will have more and more people reporting directly to you and will be asked to coordinate projects. Leaders have an impact on just about every aspect of the job. Leaders can unleash their employees' full potential by driving high performance expectations and coaching them to rise to the challenge. However, managing a team of people who look to you for guidance, instruction, development, and inspiration is no small feat. In fact, becoming an excellent leader is arguably the workplace's hardest challenge. Human beings are complicated, and it takes a range of hard and soft skills to cultivate the effective relationships that unlock top performance.

In the most literal way, being a leader means having followers. If you look back and there's nobody behind you, who cares if you're charging up a hill? But leadership is not just about managing people. It's also about shaping a company's direction, leading others to achieve the best results. It's about having the courage to stand up for your ideas. It's about your peer relationships.

If your career is progressing, leadership comes with the territory. It's hard to think of a successful career that doesn't involve leadership, regardless of your occupation or work setting.

Women's Advantage

Let's step back and look at what women face in the leadership realm, the potential hidden behind the challenges. We all know the linguistic stereotypes that plague women in leadership positions. (Men are "decisive," while women are "pushy.") As we've pointed out earlier, stereotypes about gender and leadership don't just spontaneously appear in the workplace—they're often nurtured from childhood and permeate women's lives. For example, by elementary school, girls are less likely than boys to say that their gender is smart.

A study led by Harvard professor Richard Weissbourd, head of the Making Caring Common Project, showed the impact of gender biases on teenage girls, especially in terms of leadership and power.[1] Weissbourd reported that in a pool of almost 20,000 students surveyed, only 8 percent of girls preferred that political offices be occupied by women rather than men, compared to 4 percent for boys. Only 6 percent of boys preferred that businesses be run by females. Also, mothers demonstrated a higher level of support for school councils led by boys rather than girls. In sum, boys, girls, and many parents showed an underlying discomfort with female leadership.

The good news is that gender bias in youth settings is an issue that is being aggressively addressed in literature and practice—such as in the much-praised "Like a Girl" campaign launched in 2014 by Always feminine hygiene products to empower young girls to pursue their dreams.[2] The ads featured young girls being strong in various situations, with taglines such as "I throw like a girl," "I run like a girl," and so on. #LikeAGirl has since become a movement. However, the issue of leadership isn't so often addressed.

Despite the tenacity of cultural stereotypes that take so much time to change, there's new evidence that women are rapidly outpacing men when it comes to certain key leadership qualities. In particular, women score high marks for performance in a crisis.

In a 2022 report for the *Harvard Business Review*, Jack Zenger, CEO of the leadership development consultancy Zenger Folkman, and Joseph Folkman, its president, discussed a phenomenon called the "glass cliff."[3] This occurs when companies in trouble put a woman in charge to save them, the thinking being that because the chances of success are so low, the organization has little to lose if she fails. With a poor outcome likely, they're more willing to give a woman leader a try. The glass cliff has been cited by business journalists in certain outstanding cases. For example, Emma Hinchliffe described Sue Gove's appointment as CEO of Bed Bath & Beyond that way in *Fortune*'s The Broadsheet. After a stellar career, Gove was brought on as interim CEO of the struggling company in June 2022. When chapter 11 bankruptcy was filed in April 2023, Gove took the hit. "Gove's CEO appointment is a classic example of the so-called glass cliff," Hinchliffe wrote. "Women are seen as the right choice to clean up a mess, but not to lead when times are good."[4]

Despite this imbalance in perception, Zenger and Folkman also determined that women had strong and even better leadership ratings when compared to men. Their 2019 study of over 60,000 leaders (22,603 women and 40,187 men) demonstrated women's dominance in many leadership qualities. Subsequently, Zenger and Folkman looked at similar data collected during the first phase of the COVID-19 pandemic and found that the gap between men and women leaders—in favor of women—was significantly higher than it was during ordinary times, indicating that women perform even better in a crisis.

If studies so consistently rank women as better leaders, why are there still relatively few in business leadership positions? Avivah Wittenberg-Cox, CEO of the gender consultancy 20-First and an authority on gender and business, has an interesting perspective that rings true for us. As she wrote in *Forbes*:

> Companies expect talent to fight for power. That's what men do. Women don't. They fight for purpose. That's why men sit atop the corporate world and women are now reaching the top of the public and non-profit sectors. That's also why we need more women running businesses. Male dominated companies not only underperform. They are bad for the rest of us (think tech and finance, AI and subprimes).[5]

The Making of a Mindful Leader

"There are moments that shaped me as a leader, and I'm defined by them," Kate Johnson told us. Kate, now the president and CEO of Lumen Technologies, served in major leadership roles at Microsoft, GE Digital, and Oracle, and has often reflected on what it means to be a leader. She said the "moments" she spoke of "were embedded in a combination of personal and professional circumstances. And they were so defining that I can't really imagine operating without the influences that they have."

She described four significant pivot points. The first involved developing an understanding of a growth mindset. "I learned this when my son was young. He did not fit in the standard academic world, although we knew he was very smart. I was constantly going to his school, trying to help him. His principal gave me a book by Carol Dweck called *Mindset: The New Psychology of Success.*[6] It blew my mind."

Dweck's research challenges conventional beliefs that intelligence is essentially "fixed." The fixed mindset holds that students (and anyone) can learn and achieve only to their given intelligence level. But as she began to study learning in children, Dweck found that when a growth mindset was used, which clearly stated that there were no limits to what could be learned, students became motivated to work harder and achieve their goals. The premise of a growth mindset was a revelation for Kate. "It said, you can do anything. It doesn't matter who you are, how smart you are, or what your background is. If you put the learning systems in place so that you listen and you are open to feedback and you make the modifications and you practice, practice, practice, you can do it. I started seeing progress with my son, and it helped me with everything. It helped me be a better mom, a better wife, a better professional, a better friend, a better sibling." It became the foundation of everything she did every day.

Her second pivotal leadership development moment came after she joined Microsoft. Kate was working at GE, and she was approached by Satya Nadella, the CEO of Microsoft. When they met, he asked, "Have you ever heard of growth mindset?" Satya shared that Carol Dweck had shaped him deeply as a leader and the growth mindset was the foundation of the culture that Satya aspired to build at Microsoft. That's when Kate knew she wanted to work with Satya, to be in an environment where learning and growth were valued in this way.

"Everything was different about the company we wanted to be versus the company that we were—how we made products, how we took them to market, how we supported them, how we sold. And when you have ten thousand people on your team who are basically afraid of being wrong, it's a huge problem. So it wasn't just that we had to change the mindset, we had to give them the skills and courage to get there."

To teach courage, Kate rolled out the groundbreaking approach featured in Brené Brown's *Dare to Lead* to the entire U.S. business at Microsoft. "Teaching courage involves conflict management," Kate explained. "It's how do I speak truth to power? How do I give feedback for performance management? How do I say, 'Guys, this isn't working, we've got to do something different,' and not feel like I'm the one ruining everything for everybody? Brown teaches about leaning into your values and how values drive everybody's behaviors. She talks about building trust, the boundaries, and reliability, and accountability that affect whether you're able to build trust as a team. Last, and probably most important, she teaches resilience—that is, *How do I fall over and get back up again without taking it personally, without feeling like I can't get back into the arena?*"

The third formative experience that shaped Kate as a leader happened in 2019. To accelerate team bonding at Microsoft, she'd instituted a custom of learning something together. "In May of 2019, I chose the topic of the history of race in America."

She took the team to Montgomery, Alabama, where they met with Bryan Stevenson, who'd achieved attention for his groundbreaking efforts on behalf of people on death row. His bestselling book on the topic, *Just Mercy*, had also been made into a blockbuster movie.[7]

Kate was particularly drawn to Stevenson's idea of empathy in action, which she introduced at Microsoft. In January 2020, she shut down the entire division across the country to see *Just Mercy* in theaters. It turned out to be especially important later that year when the murder of George Floyd hit the news.

Kate's fourth leadership pivot point occurred in 2021, when she decided to step away from Microsoft. At that time her children were graduating from college, her mother had passed away unexpectedly, and her dad had gone into hospice care. As Kate said, "I had transition overload."

That overload forced Kate to stop and create a self-care program, which she took very seriously. "I considered all the elements of mind, body, and soul, and sought help for both my physical and mental health, as well as my spirituality."

Through it all, she was focused on how she could create her own leadership philosophy. She studied and immersed herself in different ideas. It snapped into place for her when she took a leadership course that involved walking the Camino de Santiago in Spain. "When you walk twenty miles a day, you have to practice mindfulness because your feet are hurting, your back's hurting, your everything's hurting, and you need to separate yourself from it." Mindfulness became a regular part of her daily practice and remains so to this day.

In September 2022, Kate accepted a position as CEO at Lumen, taking with her the wisdom she'd derived from her study of Carol Dweck, Brené Brown, and Bryan Stevenson, and also from her own journey. For us, she is a living demonstration of how un-conventional learning experiences can illuminate key lessons for workplace leadership, and how bringing a mindful approach to everything you do can make you a leader others want to follow.

Designing the Kind of Leader You Want to Be

Many women—especially those who are less tenured—are ill-equipped to manage the intricacies and nuances that matter when it comes to leadership. Those who are fortunate enough to take classes on leadership or management often find that the training provides only an academic primer, not real operational skills. Leadership is best learned "on the job" by observing and experiencing a wide range of leaders as you progress in your career—although even today, many women don't have female leaders ahead of them whom they can look to as leadership role models. Women are far less likely to have a female boss at some point in their career than men are to have a male boss.

This disparity doesn't have to hold you back from developing into the leader you want to be, as long as you're intentional about it. All around you are leaders who will model effective (and sometimes less effective) behaviors. You can build your own unique vision of leadership and take advantage of formal and informal mentors to help you deliver the leadership impact you're striving for.

Christiana

The first time I managed others was as a third year in consulting. That's when you move up to be a project manager if you're high performing. I was on a team with two guys who were only a year behind me. So we had only about twelve months' difference in our experience. I thought it was really important that I stay ahead of these guys, but also that I know everything about what they were doing. I wanted to show I was in charge. I thought I needed to know exactly what the team was up to every step of the way.

One day I was looking at a financial model that one of the guys was creating. I was literally sitting behind him looking over his shoulder and I zeroed right in on the two things he needed to fix in the model. In response, he said, "You could tell me what's right with this thing before you tell me what's wrong."

Then the two of them gave me this feedback: "We feel as if you're just circling the team room saying, 'Where are you at? Where are you at? Where are you at?' Aren't there other things that you should be spending your time on?"

That's when I realized that as the manager I needed to be thinking *ahead*. I should be developing new client relationships. I had responsibilities outside the team room. I wanted to be the kind of leader who first of all acknowledged the work and wasn't just pointing out mistakes. I didn't want to be the kind of leader who was in people's faces all the time. So, that feedback from my junior colleagues made an impact on me. It was some of the best feedback on leadership I ever got.

Here are some examples of qualities and capabilities that you can prioritize and become known for as a leader in your organization:

- **Investing in people.** You take the time to guide people via coaching so they can take their contribution to the next level.
- **Supporting your team's personal lives.** You see your team

members as human beings and show that you care about how
the work is really impacting them.

- **Fostering a feedback-driven culture.** You master the art of
giving and receiving feedback so that improvement is likely to
occur regardless of the size of the task.
- **Embracing challenges in the workplace.** You maintain a
positive intent when working through problems and offer
constructive criticism.
- **Having a performance mindset and setting high expectations
that teams can rise to.** You inspire your team to want to win
and achieve *without* an "everyone gets a trophy" mindset.
- **Using humor.** You follow the lead of Stanford professor
Jennifer Aaker and lecturer Naomi Bagdonas, who teach a
course on the power of using humor to become a great leader
and have written an entire book (*Humor, Seriously*) on the
topic.[8] Humor can be a powerful tool for any leader, and a
secret weapon for women in particular. In fact, as reported
recently in the *Harvard Business Review*, research on TED
Talks and start-up pitches found that women benefit more
from being funny than men do. This is partly due to humor's
ability to convey both competence and warmth, which are
often seen as opposing, zero-sum qualities for women.[9]
- **Promoting innovation and creativity.** By your actions,
you show your belief that companies and teams can remain
competitive only if people are able to successfully innovate.
- **Earning trust and unleashing empowerment.** You reward
teams and individuals who establish a track record of
performing year over year.

As with just about anything in life, you'll get better results if you're
intentional. Here are some qualities to try to cultivate in yourself:

- Integrity
- Empathy
- Fairness
- Directness and transparency
- Authenticity
- Accountability
- Ability to listen well
- Gratitude
- Recognition of impact and effort

These traits will especially stand you in good stead when you are leading work teams. You need a mix of approachability and toughness to manage the sometimes-touchy conversations that are necessary in work settings.

You can begin by consciously thinking about the kind of leader you want to be and recognizing that your leadership identity is going to develop over time. A Career Forward mindset helps you be more aware of your leadership skills and opportunities.

Be sure to call on people you trust to serve as sounding boards. Here we're not talking about mentors but rather about colleagues who'll give it to you straight and tell you if you're not measuring up. There's always room to grow, so use this feedback for intentional leadership development.

As you progress in your career, you might not see leaders who perfectly model your vision or style. That's okay. Take from them what you can. Christiana once worked for a partner who was a genius at defusing tensions with directness and aplomb. Rather than simply admiring him, she paid attention to exactly what he said, how he said it, and in what situations he spoke. Then she practiced this in her own way until it came naturally. Her new skill came in handy when she forgot a meeting with an important client. When he called to rightfully chew her out, she picked up the phone and said, "Let me have it," disarming the client and giving her a chance to apologize without escalating tensions.

There are endless leadership profiles and an abundance of advice about the top leadership characteristics. Many of these portraits are based on traditional models or hierarchal power-based leadership. You don't have to adopt those styles, which might feel outdated, inauthentic, or ineffective—not to mention mostly written with men in mind. Approach the question of leadership identity with an awareness that you're writing your own story.

Be a discerning observer. When you observe something that you admire, take time to learn and incorporate it into your own toolkit. Use the NAP method, which is simply notice, adapt, and practice. Keep the acronym in your back pocket and use it regularly. We find this one of the most effective and engaging ways to design your unique leadership style and develop into the best boss you can be.

Having said that, developing your leadership identity isn't merely a matter of picking qualities you admire in others. It's very much about being true to yourself—a quality that is consistently found in great leaders.

No one can be everything to everyone, and that's not what's expected from you. Furthermore, cookie-cutter approaches to leadership typically don't work because people are so different. But if you can be strategic and identify a few key principles that you deeply believe in and integrate them into your leadership skill set, you'll not only find success but also be authentic doing so.

At the same time, recall your special differentiator from chapter 7. This is the quality that sets you apart and informs your career success. Don't be afraid to lean into it.

And don't forget that your boss, peers, and direct reports can offer valuable insights about how you operate at work. As you develop your leadership capability and philosophy, be open about communicating with your team. Tell them what you care about and which programs you'd like to develop. This creates an atmosphere of transparency, authenticity, and accountability, and helps them feel like valued members of your team.

Grace

I learned the value of having a mental model and using visualization. The mental model I relied on involved acknowledging that I was in a state of continuous learning and awareness. I liked to visualize capturing new traits or gaining new insights and putting them in a treasure chest. When that happened, it was like an active "note to self." Then I could pull out one or two items and start actively practicing them. In this way, the treasure in my chest was constantly growing.

Finding the Right Mentors for Your Style

In addition to identifying role models to look to for inspiration, you must have mentors who can provide candid feedback, advice, and support. This is a prerequisite for becoming a truly exceptional leader, and it requires a more strategic approach than simply picking mentors from senior leadership. Just because someone has a title higher than yours doesn't mean they're the right fit as a mentor. What makes mentorship relationships work—and endure—is chemistry. There must be an intellectual or personal connection, as well as mutual respect, which encourages a bond to form. The honest conversations that spring from that often lead to exponential improvements.

Mentors can be found both inside and outside our organizations. They work in all industries, and the good ones see a little of themselves in aspiring leaders and are committed to helping them thrive.

Christiana

When I got hired as an executive at Nike, one of the best pieces of advice I received was from one of the co-presidents. He told me to make sure I had someone who'd tell me if I was standing in the path of a bus that was barreling down the road about to hit me. Although this metaphor might be a bit off-putting, it really resonated with me, because that's what it can feel like to be blindsided by something as a new leader.

My previous work was valuable, but it was impossible for me to come into a new environment and understand all the nuances in culture and communications. Clearly, if I had someone who'd proactively tell me if I was about to get run over, it would make a huge difference in my success.

Luckily my boss, Jeanne Jackson, fulfilled that role. She'd brought me in from consulting and had been a longtime mentor and supporter. I knew that expanding my internal network would also be critical, so I focused on getting to know other leaders in the company. I went out of my way to cultivate relationships and pay it forward to help others. This set the wheels in motion for productive conversations, teamwork, and support. A decade later, I'm still great friends with many of those executives.

Here are some tips for finding mentors:

- **Formal relationships:** Don't be afraid to ask people directly for help. In our experience, women are more hesitant to do this than men are. When you approach someone to be your mentor, it's smart to say why you're asking *them* rather than another leader. Be specific about what you admire in them and what you'd like to learn from them. Propose parameters on how you'd like to meet with your mentor and say that you'll come to these meetings prepared with targeted questions. This puts the responsibility on your shoulders, making it easier for your mentor to help.

- **Informal relationships:** Rather than formally asking people to mentor you, another option is to simply build relationships with people who are your role models. Ask to be on projects they're leading, attend their work seminars, volunteer for extracurricular projects, or introduce yourself at company events. Also, ask colleagues to introduce you.

- **Know that your mentors will change over time:** You can maintain your relationships with mentors, but there will likely be a limit to the knowledge they can provide. As your career grows and evolves and you find yourself focusing on a certain niche, you should connect with someone else who has specialized knowledge in what you need to learn. Remember that people will come in and out of your life for a reason.

As you advance in your career, never forget that the most magnetic leaders are the ones who have strong teams that shine and are viewed as top performers with high potential for growth. As they climb, these leaders pull up other top performers who are in demand. In the end, a leader's success shows through the quality of the team's capability and performance.

And there's one more important point we want to make— something you may not have heard before. Being a leader— helping other people do good work, develop, and grow—is *fun*. It's rewarding to lead a team that puts numbers on the board for the company, and it's enjoyable to celebrate successes and gain team recognition. And it's inspiring to watch people you've led succeed as a result of your mentorship.

· · · · ·

Individually in our careers we each reached the "Aha!" moment of realizing that we'd much rather take all the challenges that came with leadership than not have the challenges and be in the back row. This is the essence of leading full lives and embracing the Career Forward mindset.

KEY TAKEAWAYS

- Women make superior leaders, notably in times of crisis or change.

- There is no single type of leadership model.
  Be true to yourself.

- Cultivate authentic connections with mentors, even when you're in a more senior role.

- Leadership is a constant learning process. Use a growth mindset to continue your development.

12

Own Your Ambition

Be bold. If you're going to make an error, make a doozy,
and don't be afraid to hit the ball.

—Billie Jean King

As we thought about the question of women and ambition, we imagined how we'd talk about it if we were speaking to our own daughters. What message would we want to send? How would we tell them to own their ambition, to get comfortable with it? It's not always easy to talk about female ambition. How could we address it in a way that would break through all the negative connotations that have been built up over the decades?

First, we want to start from this position: it's totally okay to be ambitious. We believe it's a key to unlocking empowerment and competitive advantage for Career Forward women. Our message is straightforward: own your ambition and be bold about it.

Female Ambition Doesn't Need to Be Silent

Even today, if you research the topic of women and ambition, few resources take a wholeheartedly pro-ambition position. Most are devoted to showing why openly ambitious women get a bum rap.

No wonder younger women are often cautious when it comes to expressing their appetite for career progression! *Business Insider* found that 59 percent of women they polled said that having ambition was an important trait for career success,[1] and 50 percent of the women said they identified as ambitious. However, only about a third felt comfortable actually *calling* themselves ambitious. *Business Insider* cited one reason being the likability trap: women are encouraged to be likable to advance their careers, yet likability is often viewed as being in conflict with female ambition.

In our society, whether the arena is business, politics, academia, or other front-facing careers, women can pay a steep price for ambition. In 2017, *Forbes* published a list of headlines that had been written about Hillary Clinton during her presidential run: "Is Hillary Clinton Pathologically Ambitious?" "Flip-Flops Show Clinton Is Long on Ambition, Short on Principles." "Hillary Clinton's Unbridled Ambition Trips Her Up Again." "Don't Destroy the Dems to Satisfy Clinton's Ambition." "The Curse of Hillary Clinton's Ambition."[2]

You don't have to be a partisan to notice that there's something wrong with this picture. *Forbes* pointed out that we'd be hard-pressed to find such headlines written about a male candidate. Why? Because "handing over power to men—whether earned or not—is the default."

It's not just likability that's an underlying issue. The bias against ambitious women also might be caused by their perceived threat. The Boston Consulting Group surveyed 200,000 employees—141,000 women—from 189 countries and found that at the start of their careers (under age thirty) women's levels of ambition matched men's. However, by the time women were in their thirties and forties—especially in firms that weren't progressive on gender diversity—only 66 percent of women sought promotions, compared with 87 percent of men.[3]

This ambition gap virtually disappeared in settings that were more gender diverse in leadership. The conclusion was that given an environment where ambition in women is valued, women will step up.

It's probably fair to say that many women are *silently* ambitious. They construct their career plans while staying under the radar. They hesitate to step out into the spotlight and make a power play.

Christiana

When I was a second-year associate in management consulting, I was dating someone who'd worked for the same firm. I felt uncomfortable talking to him about how well I was doing and how much I enjoyed consulting. When he asked me once if I wanted to try to make partner at the firm, I instantly denied it, but in reality I was very interested in succeeding on that path. In hindsight, I was definitely "silently ambitious" for a good deal of my early career years, and only began to openly express my career goals later as I realized that stating my aspirations clearly to my bosses—and myself!—spurred me to pursue those goals with much greater focus. Looking back, I wish I had the confidence earlier to say what I wanted to achieve and own my ambition openly.

So where do we land on the role of ambition in a Career Forward context? We believe there's a real power that comes from declaring your ambition and stating your intent. People take note, and it gets factored into decisions. Men do this all the time. You'll hear, "He expects to be CEO in five years," and everyone nods with approval and gives him challenging assignments.

When women are silent about what they want to achieve and the importance of work in their lives, it is assumed that they lack ambition. Confidence and being comfortable in her own skin can help a woman muster the courage to express her ambition.

Tory Burch, the executive chairman and chief creative officer of her own brand, Tory Burch LLC, talked about this phenomenon in an essay for LinkedIn in 2016: "In my *first interview* with *The New York Times* in 2004, when the reporter mentioned the word 'ambitious,' I commented that the word annoyed me . . . I realized that I had bought into the stigma that women shouldn't be ambitious—that it was unattractive somehow. In men, it is a compliment and in women it's used negatively. But that's a harmful double standard that we must overcome for women to achieve parity in the workplace."[4]

When we asked Kate Johnson about her early experiences with the idea of ambition, she had powerful childhood memories. "I grew up in an Irish Catholic family," she said. "There were four kids, and my parents were focused on two things, humility and grace.

"But I was bold and brash, and different than my siblings." Kate couldn't remember a time when she didn't have a vision—when she didn't want to compete and win. It didn't matter if the arena was sports, school, or work. "But I had to learn to play the game of keeping that quiet," she admitted. "And I'm not sure it was a terrible thing, given the generation that I'm in. Because bold and brash was not accepted in the early 1990s and 2000s. Although I had no guiding light from my home, I had a great education. I got an engineering degree, but I was not a good engineer. I'd thought it was what I wanted to do from an early age, but I realized that I was probably better at being sort of the translator for technology rather than the creator of technology. So I went into tech sales." Kate's career took an upward swing from there, because she had the courage to get in the ring and find her true path, and not be dissuaded from expressing her ambition.

If you feel caught in a negative mindset, we encourage you to redefine ambition for yourself. Reject the labels. Celebrate the advantages.

Change the words; change the mindset:

NEGATIVE FRAMING	POSITIVE REDEFINITION
"She's aggressive"	"She's industrious"
"She's power-hungry"	"She's goal-oriented"
"She's full of herself"	"She's confident"
"She's pushy"	"She's determined"
"She's overambitious"	"She's motivated"
"She's opportunistic"	"She's intentional"
"She's bossy"	"She's decisive"

The Great Thing About Ambition

When you have a strong desire to achieve, it stimulates the actions required to build a successful long-term career. Ambition can lead you to take chances, to learn more. It helps you become the best version of yourself. When you're ambitious, you'll work toward larger goals. You'll feel proud of your accomplishments.

The three qualities that get mentioned the most when career professionals talk about ambition are hard work, dedication, and perseverance. These are Career Forward qualities. We'll add high performance to those three because hard work, dedication, and perseverance say nothing about your actual impact. Being good at what you do is a big part of ambition. Otherwise, it's just noise.

Having ambition gets you a bump for all those reasons, but being bold and visibly owning it will turbocharge those benefits.

It's satisfying to repaint the picture of what ambition means. It's a real motivator. Ambitious people expose themselves to new ways of thinking. They make choices that are personally bold.

Being bold is about your own self-empowerment. It's about perspective. Boldness rejects the victim mentality: "I've got to fight to have my voice." Rather, it's a tool that enables you to speak up without anxiety about what you're worth, what you want, and what consideration you've earned. This is a personal gut check. You might not look bold to others, but that doesn't matter. What matters is what it looks like for you.

Sometimes people get confused about what it means to be bold in a professional setting. They think they must charge full speed ahead and take actions that cause others to sit up and take notice. Not so. The kind of boldness we're talking about is an inner quality that gives you the confidence to express your ambition, even when you face challenges. It's the sense of confidence that tells you you're on the right course—that you've got it handled. There are few things as professionally rewarding as knowing yourself and being able to show what you've got.

Let Your Light Shine

When you express your ambition and aspire to rise during your career, you don't hide your light under a bushel. Once you embrace your ambition, your motivation to grow might become stronger than ever. Earlier, we talked about women questioning their ambition and dropping out. That pullback often occurs at a point of transition when, if they were just a bit bolder, their career progression would take them into senior leadership. We're going to tell you how to make it through—and also why it's important that you do. It's a moment when all the lessons of Career Forward come into play.

Having a senior role is a big deal, especially at a large organization. Out of hundreds, thousands, or tens of thousands of people, there are only a handful of individuals at the top who are responsible for making key decisions that affect the workforce and other stakeholders. It's a job with a lot of responsibilities and long hours, but we believe it's worth it—even with the hard work and the trade-offs.

To be sure, a senior role will call on you to grow and contribute in new ways. That's because you'll no longer be focusing your time solely on your function or area. For example, if you're a VP of marketing who gets promoted to chief marketing officer, you'll be leading global marketing efforts for the company, but you'll also be pulled into many enterprise-level decisions *outside* of marketing. In fact, you can probably expect about 40 percent of your time to be dedicated to learning about other issues across the company and helping to resolve them. This might include company strategy, culture, operations, sales, product development, and more. Executives are expected to contribute in all senior team meetings, understand what's going on, and help make decisions.

This means you'll be immediately placed outside your comfort zone. Knowing this ahead of time will help prevent you from being caught off guard when you find yourself at a new level of responsibility. The more you can learn in advance about how the company functions, its consumers and stakeholders, and the keys to its success, the faster you can contribute your perspectives. Being able to take a seat at the leadership table with confidence and show you have a point of view makes a huge difference in starting out strong.

Five Top Job Truths

After holding senior roles ourselves and speaking with our women peers about what it takes to succeed as an executive, we identified five factors that are key elements of long-term success. We call them the Five Top Job Truths. We wish these truths had been shared with us when we were first promoted into senior roles, and we share them here so you can reflect and apply the lessons as they become relevant to your journey. These are evergreen topics that are relevant today and will be relevant tomorrow as you grow into new roles and explore new opportunities.

1. **Prioritize relationships and collaboration.** The higher you progress in your field, the more you're required to collaborate. This might seem counterintuitive because all the language of career growth and promotions involves rising above others. However, every leadership role we've ever been in has involved intense collaboration. There is a high level of interdependency in support functions and teams, and everyone relies on others to get things done effectively. The great news is that women are often socialized growing up to be more collaborative—a real advantage as a senior leader. The neuroscience says that women tend to use collaborative, participative, and transformational leadership styles more than men.[5]

   The most successful companies have highly collaborative senior leadership teams who leverage one another's strengths and expertise for the benefit of the company—which is why you should plan on prioritizing relationships with your fellow executives. Do as much as you can to get to know your colleagues on a personal level, use their help and insights, and be proactive about recognizing the value of the collective leadership team expertise. It's also important to understand the needs and ambitions of your peers so you can both understand their motivations *and* build relationship equity by supporting them in achieving their career goals. Strong peer relationships and collaborations can raise all boats.

2. **The company dynamic matters.** Every company has a culture and company dynamics. And yes, there *are* company politics. At the unhealthy extreme, certain people wield more power than they should, and decisions are made in an opaque way. This can hinder a team's ability to reach its full potential and leave some team members feeling annoyed, insecure, and unmotivated.

    If you find yourself in this kind of situation, our best advice is to recognize it and make choices to move in another direction. This is not the kind of executive culture you want to be a part of, and there are plenty of opportunities at other companies that would provide a healthier work environment.

    Still, it's important to understand that all companies have unique working environments where some of these dynamics will exist. After all, companies are made up of individuals with different career objectives, interpersonal skills, and value systems. Even when teams are filled with nothing but pleasant, high-functioning people, some teammates will be more influential than others. Some will have closer relationships and go the extra mile to help others. Aside from that, there will always be a history of company decisions that went well or didn't, and those results can leave a lasting impression on leaders.

    As a rising executive, you need to be a student of corporate dynamics. Try to learn as much as you can about how decisions are made at the executive level, and who the key influencers are in various situations. Listen and learn about these dynamics even as you continue to develop in your current role.

One of the best things you can do is to try to read between the lines of what is said in formal meetings. Are certain colleagues always chatting in the hallway afterward? Does one person often seem to echo or second what another leader says? Is there an individual who seems to be exceptionally well-liked by the other leaders or the CEO? These elements play a factor in how decisions are made and where power is shifting among team members.

Another great way to read the tea leaves is to leverage your relationships with peers. Invite another leader to coffee, and make sure you do more listening than talking. You might be surprised to learn the backstory on certain things that have happened in the company, and how the effects are still being felt in various subtle ways. Little tidbits of information can do wonders to help you understand dynamics that you might be picking up on but don't fully understand.

Learn who to talk to and how to frame information to gain support and drive the outcomes you want. Staying connected to the beat of the organization and shifts in the power base will help you navigate and accomplish more within the company. Time and time again, the candid information we've gleaned from informal conversations has made all the difference in our being effective in our roles.

3. **Communication must happen "at scale."** As part of leadership, you serve as a representative of the company. You may have to communicate with a diverse set of stakeholders,

including the board, managers, your functional team, the entire staff as a whole, and even potentially the press. Sometimes you'll be talking with a handful of individuals you know well, and other times it could be thousands of employees. The topics you'll need to speak on will be broader than what you've dealt with before, and people will ask you about parts of the business that aren't your core expertise. Further, you'll need to become adept at addressing controversial subjects that require careful consideration and exactness in messaging.

This is what we call leadership communication "at scale," and you will want to learn to do it well and with your own style. It's a crucial part of the job. If you aren't used to being in the spotlight or don't particularly love the idea of being thrust into it, this is something you should work on getting comfortable with. There are also technical skills you may need to learn, including reading from a teleprompter, memorizing scripted remarks, and handling media questions. Once you're in leadership, you're assumed to be speaking for the organization when you talk, and eyes are always on you.

In addition to formally structured communications, you'll need to be able to communicate well on the fly. Carrie Cox is an established executive leader in the biopharmaceutical industry, both in operating roles and as a corporate director. She is currently chairman of Organon, a women's health spin-off of Merck & Co., and was named to *Fortune*'s list of the 50 Most Powerful Women in Business six times. Carrie says that being able to maintain composure in difficult situations has served her incredibly well over the years. "Train yourself to stay calm in stressful environments," she said. "It is not easy to do, but you need to find a way to react calmly in crisis situations. This ensures you have a clearer mind to make decisions in the moment, and helps others stay focused and strong as well."

We know that as an executive, your ability to stay composed will be tested continuously. Getting emotional in the workplace will not lead to an effective result. Unfortunately, this is one of those situations where men tend to get the benefit of the doubt and women don't. If a man gets worked up on the job, people might excuse him by saying that he got caught up in the moment or is extra passionate. If a woman gets worked up, people are more likely to see it as a red flag. It isn't fair, but it's a common bias. So when you choose how to react to an unfair situation, remember that it's not worth becoming labeled as emotional. We like the mantra: "Keep calm and carry on." Staying poised when you're put to the test (which will undoubtedly happen over your career) will inspire confidence across your team and with your peers.

4. **Many of your peers will be men.** The higher you climb in your career, the more likely you are to find yourself surrounded by men. Of course, that will vary by industry and profession, but on average, women make up just under half of the workforce, yet hold only 25 percent of senior executive positions at U.S. public companies. This skew is true across professions. For example,

- In the legal profession, women are 45 percent of associates but only 22.7 percent of partners.
- In medicine, women represent 40 percent of all physicians and surgeons but only 16 percent of permanent medical school deans.

- In academia, women have earned the majority of doctorates for eight consecutive years but are only 32 percent of full professors.[6]

The gender gap is slowly improving, but women are still grossly underrepresented in top roles.

Depending on your company and industry, you might frequently be the only woman in the room at meetings. Sometimes this isn't a big deal, but other times it can feel uncomfortable, isolating, or intimidating. In our experience as the only women in numerous rooms, we felt like we had the responsibility to "represent" to the best of our abilities. First and foremost, we knew that in demonstrating how highly capable we were, we could help pave the way for more female leaders to walk in our footsteps.

We know this "pressure to model" is true for other underrepresented groups—not just women—who are all too familiar with taking on the extra weight of representing an entire group of people, whether they want to or not. It's helpful to anticipate this and look for opportunities to develop your response before starting your role.

It's also entirely likely that you will find your male colleagues looking to you for the "woman's perspective" on various issues. Offering your perspective can be helpful, but it's also important to realize that it should not be your sole responsibility to be the voice for women or for any specific group in your company. If you find yourself feeling put in that situation, be open with your colleagues about how more diverse voices will be beneficial, and how other senior executives have the responsibility to be allies for women, not just you.

Related to this, each of us often found ourselves being the only person in the room speaking up and asking about the pipeline of female candidates for various positions. When this began happening regularly, we realized we needed to ask our peers whether diversity was important to the company. The fact that we asked the question (to which the answer should be a loud yes) reminded our colleagues that they *also* should be speaking up to be sure the organization was developing diverse talent.

Christiana

On my first executive team trip, we had an overnight flight on the company plane. I wasn't exactly sure how the sleeping arrangements would work. In my consulting life, we slept sitting up if we took red-eye flights, but I heard that things were different on the jet. When it started getting late, the flight attendant turned each pair of seats into a comfy bed, and I realized we were all going to be lying down sleeping next to each other. As the only woman on the flight, I had no idea what the "bedtime" protocol was going to be, so I waited as my colleagues headed one after another to the restroom to get ready to bed down for the night.

Luckily, I wasn't surrounded by a bunch of guys in their shorts, as it turned out that everyone had brought some version of Nike sweats to wear. However, I was still unprepared for the intimacy of sleeping directly next to coworkers. It wasn't something I'd ever considered when taking the executive role, but thankfully, the awkwardness I felt wore off quickly. My colleagues kept it professional, and waking up among coworkers with bed head after our overnight flights became a routine part of the job.

5. **Continuous growth is the name of the game.** Sometimes people think that once they reach a certain level, they have arrived. They've found the pot of gold at the end of the rainbow, and it's nothing but sunshine and good fortune from there on out. But that isn't how ambition works. Continuing to grow and progress requires you to be constantly in a mode of contributing and achieving—for this year, and the next, and the one after that. You must keep adding value. That's what it takes to keep the job. There are always leaders coming up behind you who are hungry for those roles.

   Over the years, we've heard numerous CEOs talk about the need for "fresh blood" in various positions. This has always caught our attention because we know one of the challenges companies face is that leadership can become complacent. It's a reality that executives who stop reinventing themselves can be at risk of being managed out of the company.

   Remember that the skills and capabilities that elevated you to your current position aren't enough to keep you growing. If you aren't boosting your knowledge and competencies, you're losing competitive ground. For example, building digital skills is becoming more and more important. In many companies, it's an imperative for executives. We've seen leaders who weren't able to make the shift to digital, and they became less relevant over time.

   If you focus on continuous growth throughout your career—as an essential Career Forward strategy—it will be easier for you to stay in that mode as you transition into higher jobs. There are plenty of things you can do to keep honing your capabilities. Speak at conferences, write articles, and learn from colleagues and mentors. Do things that take you outside your comfort zone. If you feel like you're stretching yourself, you know you're doing something right.

Grace

Over my career journey, I chose opportunities to stretch myself by working in very different industries. These included positions of increasing responsibilities in technology, consumer products, aviation, and food and beverage companies. By doing so, I was exposed to different cultures, business practices, and leadership styles.

Ultimately, your goal may be to reach a top leadership level in your chosen field—whether it be corporate, academic, creative, medical, or some other focus. We encourage you not to shirk from being ambitious—in fact, to embrace the possibility. If you own your ambition, are passionate about your work, and keep performing at a higher and higher level, you'll find yourself in challenging and significant roles.

For each of us, becoming an executive has been a highly rewarding experience, and we strongly recommend pursuing it. But the journey probably would have been easier if we'd had a better idea of what to expect, knew how to prepare for what was ahead, and fully comprehended the joy and satisfaction that was in store for us. When title, money, and recognition finally come together in a way that confirms you're at the top, you may at last feel that you've arrived. In reality, it's a much more complicated milestone, but now that you know the challenges you'll encounter when you achieve a senior position, you'll be better able to prepare for what's ahead.

KEY TAKEAWAYS

- Embrace the A-word.

- It's not easy to be "the only" in a room, but it's likely to be your reality at various points in your career.

- There will always be a premium on keeping calm and carrying on, especially in tough situations.

- Practice boldness until it's a comfortable tool in your professional kit.

13 ▶

Meet the Moment

In our most difficult moments, we are given an opportunity
to reset and determine who we are or want to be.
You alone shape your life.

—Megan Hine, survival consultant, author, and television presenter

September 11, 2001, was an ordinary day for both of us.
Christiana was at home near Los Angeles, three hours
behind New York, when the Twin Towers fell. She remembers
waking up and turning on the news, as she always did, only to
watch the second tower collapse. She was instantly on high alert.
McKinsey emailed colleagues to tell them not to come in, since
no one knew if the attacks were limited to the East Coast or
might spread to other big cities like LA. Christiana's ten-year-
old son, Tim, was glued to the TV, and was soon notified that
school had been canceled for the day.

Within hours, it was clear that members of the McKinsey
consulting teams Christiana was leading, spread across California, Arizona, and Idaho, were stranded, as all flights were canceled. The rest of that day was largely a blur of trying to find
ways to get colleagues home (rental cars, buses, trains, and anything with wheels was fair game) and participating in endless

conference calls, which were still a relatively new technology at the time. Business travel was impossible for weeks, personal hygiene on the road was an exercise in creativity for over a year (for example, *How long can I go without fresh contact lens solution if I can't bring any liquids in my bag?*), and conference calls became a typical, though less effective, alternative to in-person meetings. It was clear to Christiana that the way she and her consulting colleagues worked was undergoing permanent change.

Grace was working for Kraft at the time, and the morning of 9/11 she was outside her office at a supplier location in Chicago. When the news came, she stood with others in the common area and watched as the towers fell and crowds of people desperately fled for their lives. She rushed home to her children, ages eight and eleven, who were worried that their father, traveling overseas, was safe. Grace reassured them that he was an experienced global traveler and had the skills to maneuver difficult situations. While she calmed her children, Grace found herself consumed with what lay ahead. For the first time in history, all air travel in the United States was stopped, with planes randomly landing at the nearest airports.

The skies were quiet and the market was closed, but Grace was engaged and on high alert. She took full inventory of where each of her team members was, tracing their locations to make sure they were safe. This wasn't an easy process, because keeping track of everyone's location wasn't generally done at the time. In the process of connecting, Grace witnessed tremendous acts of resilience and collaboration, such as people who were stuck in New York renting cars and driving all the way back to Chicago. This spirit would continue in countless ways during the coming days and weeks.

Grace lived close to an airport, and one of her strongest memories is of lying in bed that first night and hearing fighter jets fly over the house. It was an unnerving and stark reminder of America's vulnerability.

September 11 presented a moment of crisis that affected the entire nation and the world. It had a deeply emotional impact, and it also ushered in tremendous change. Reflecting on our own experiences and speaking with others, we all felt that things would never be the same.

As leaders in our companies, we had to find ways for our teams to communicate and execute plans during a period when plane travel was limited or extremely difficult. Each airport visit involved standing in long lines, with waits sometimes for hours, as new security measures were launched. We witnessed the different ways leaders responded. In some cases, people tried to resume previous ways of working—an attempt to normalize things during a very scary and unpredictable time. That approach failed, though, because the ground had already shifted underfoot and there was no normal to return to.

Looking back, we can see the ways we were tiptoeing into new technology. The teleconferencing that was such a breakthrough two decades later during the pandemic was virtually nonexistent, but we were all trying to find ways of communicating across distances. We began to rethink our priorities, and we saw that some of the travel everyone took for granted was perhaps unnecessary. We could feel the shift to remote communication being born, even though it didn't fully emerge until the pandemic.

The shared experience of *9/11* and the changes that have taken place over the years since have made an impact most people can recognize—even if they were very young at the time. In general, however, you might be asking yourself whether women like us who started our careers thirty-plus years ago can really understand and relate to what you're experiencing now. Times have changed so much. Could the wisdom we've acquired over the years still be relevant for women today, given current challenges and circumstances Our short answer is an emphatic yes.

As it turns out, although the times and circumstances may change, the fundamentals stay the same. Every generation will experience events that are so momentous they change the world, as well as the way people work. How you meet these moments—and use change as an opportunity to grow as a professional—will define how well you're able to move forward in your career. Meeting the moment in a Career Forward way means accepting the inevitability of major change while, first, holding steady to your key principles and purpose, and second, leveraging change as an opportunity for professional growth.

If you have a long career, you'll experience a number of change moments, but the big ones are rarer. The events that took place around *9/11* constituted such a moment. So did the COVID pandemic. Once again, a completely unexpected event shook us to the bones—in many ways because of its direct and long-term consequences for the workplace. Our message is to embrace new realities without fear. This is the essence of resilience, an essential tool in a successful career.

Trials and Triumphs

Change is always with us. The ancient Greek philosopher Heraclitus is credited with saying, "Change is the only constant in life." The future won't be like the past. It never is. If it seems like the pace of change has accelerated in our times, that's because it has, and it can be dizzying. Part of the current transformation was triggered by the COVID-19 pandemic, but we don't believe the pandemic was responsible for *creating* the disruption. Rather, trends that were already developing speeded up because of the pandemic.[1] Those trends involve workplaces becoming less hierarchical, more flexible, and more diverse.

The pandemic was highly disruptive for some industries, leading to massive layoffs in travel, hospitality, retail, and all the support industries around offices. Leaders had to figure out how to pivot and work remotely. These would have been unthinkable circumstances in earlier times, but even given advanced modern technology, the circumstances were still unfamiliar and coping with them required agility. Yet people rose to the occasion.

We've often talked about how creativity is fundamental to career success. The workplace pandemic response was a massive exercise in creativity and resilience. Leaders and workers alike were forced to collaborate on solutions involving different ways to work and communicate, new methods of managing manufacturing and supply chains, and different methods for reaching customers and clients. Sometimes these approaches were successful; other times, companies struggled as people figured it out. The pandemic brought a lot of stress to the workplace.

But there were positive changes as well. As we all found ourselves meeting the moment, there were transformative experiences and innovations that have become a part of the way we live and work. Often these grew out of the pressure that companies were feeling—in effect, turning a negative into a positive.

In our experience, this level of pressure can help to build resilience and lead to professional and personal growth. Such pressure has happened for us not just in times of crisis but also in boom times when more was demanded. During the pandemic we saw how many companies struggled, but the workers who coped with those trials experienced higher levels of empowerment and satisfaction.

It has been especially exciting to see certain creative solutions emerge in a more permanent way as a result of the pandemic. For example, telehealth has been a roaring success, making non-emergency doctor visits much more possible, and it's doubtful telehealth would ever have become a common practice were it not for the pandemic.

Like health, education has also undergone a transformation, with more colleges and professional institutions offering online learning in a more engaging atmosphere—perfect for aspiring leaders who want to learn new skills.

In communications, Zoom video calls became an essential professional and personal connector, a technique that has retained its value, allowing more frequent check-ins and saving companies thousands and even millions in expenses that were once devoted to travel and meetings—especially conferences. As companies explore the best models of in-person vs. remote work to suit their cultures and their needs, videoconferencing will no doubt retain a prominent place. Obviously, Zoom calls don't replace personal interactions with families and friends, but they're a reliable substitute when distance and circumstances keep people physically apart.

From "Quiet Quitting" to "Quiet Hiring"

So what does all this change mean for you? Major disruptions in the status quo will have consequences. As we were writing this book, some big worker movements were sweeping across the internet and social media. The remote work during the pandemic opened up a nationwide conversation about how the workplace has traditionally been structured. "The Great Resignation" and "quiet quitting" trended, with workers leaving jobs or limiting their commitments. These movements often got characterized as workers being unwilling to go the extra mile for their careers. But under the surface, there's a deeper dynamic at work.

Data shows that the primary reason for the high rate of resignations was the search for more rewarding and better-paying jobs. According to the Pew Research Center, the primary reasons people left their jobs in 2021 were low pay, no opportunity for advancement, and feeling disrespected.[2] In other words, they weren't so much quitting as they were advocating for themselves. For this reason, the Great Resignation is also referred to as the Great Reshuffle. That's a positive shift, involving people rethinking their career choices. In deciding to make a move, they were doing what we talked about—finding their true purpose and realizing that great joy and satisfaction can come from pursuing a career that fits them. It's especially telling that the majority of workers who quit their jobs in this phase were under thirty—an age when people are looking to discover what's important to them.

Social media can elevate topics far beyond their actual importance, and we think that happened with quiet quitting. Quiet quitting took social media by storm with the declaration that millions of workers (especially millennials and Gen Z) were choosing to do their jobs and only their jobs—not going above or beyond. It wasn't really quitting, just downsizing their commitment to work.[3] The knee-jerk reaction in many quarters was that millennials and Gen Z were opting out of being serious about their careers. We see it differently.

Younger workers are setting markers that might ultimately be positive for productivity and career satisfaction. For example, think about boundaries. When we were coming up in our careers, nobody talked about boundaries. It wasn't necessarily a healthy situation, but people who wanted to advance in their careers didn't feel free to challenge norms. Now people are legitimately asking how a committed career can also involve legitimate boundaries.

The pandemic exposed for many people how much they were compromising their lives and fulfillment in what felt like *24/7* work crushes. Now workers—especially young workers—are taking a stand and saying, "I'm not going back to compromising what's important to me and yielding to a *24/7* job expectation." In the long run, this might be a healthy adaptation. And remember, not every worker is a careerist. Individuals are free to choose where work fits in their lives.

In 2023, the landscape shifted again as companies reevaluated workforce priorities. According to *Forbes*, companies have started to quietly encourage the development of new skills without bringing in new employees. The emerging trend has been dubbed "quiet hiring" as a nod to "quiet quitting," although no actual hiring goes on. In fact, that's the point. Increasingly, companies are upskilling their existing workforces to help fill critical positions, rather than looking outside.

This is good news for Career Forward–oriented workers who want to upgrade their skills and take advantage of new opportunities to grow within their companies. While quiet quitting challenged many aspects of a Career Forward focus, Aditya Malik writes in *Forbes* that "quiet hiring" underscores the potential of the right kind of career focus, with a "positive work culture that encourages communication, transparency and employee feedback."[4]

Tips: 5 Ways to Upskill in Challenging Times

Upskilling means advancing your skills with training opportunities, such as tech learning. (According to the National Skills Coalition, one in three workers have limited digital skills.) Upskilling is especially important during periods of change when companies are reorganizing and downsizing. Be prepared to show your value to an organization by doing the following:

1) **Identify the gaps.** Do a serious evaluation of your skills as they apply to the needs and opportunities in your company or division. Where might a new skill set or knowledge base help you grow in your company or increase your value on the job market?

2) **Sign up to learn.** There are plenty of opportunities online, such as LinkedIn Learning and Skillshare. Do your homework and make a commitment to incorporate at least one educational opportunity into your weekly schedule.

3) **Follow the thought leaders.** Never before has so much top-level advice been so readily available. For example, TED Talks has a whole library of inspirational leaders you can watch on your laptop or phone.

4) **Listen to grow.** When you're in your car, doing laundry, or working out, listen to podcasts that teach and motivate.

5) **Show your stuff.** Don't just absorb new knowledge and ideas. Find ways to put your learning into action. When the opportunity comes, do something different or surprising, and let your boss know that you learned it in a class or a thought leader advised it in a TED Talk. Your boss will be impressed by your motivation and might tag you for more formal learning opportunities.

Navigating the Transitions

We're not saying that change isn't scary. Unexpected crises over which you have no control can upend your career path. Job insecurity in the aftermath of the pandemic is a real phenomenon. We can't just say, "Don't worry, you can overcome anything." Empty words don't help. What we can do is show you ways to meet the moment no matter where you are in your career. As we've talked to colleagues and peers in various industries, we've gathered practical advice for some of the most common scenarios you might face in a time of change.

Situation 1: Your division has experienced layoffs, and your boss expects the remaining staff to take on the extra load of those who've departed—without a change in salary or title.

This is a common situation when there are layoffs. You can stave off the extra uncompensated workload by being proactive. Think of it as an opportunity to increase your value as part of the team. Approach your boss early in the layoff process and ask for specific areas of responsibility that may come up for reassignment. Look for those that appeal to your special interest or expertise, or which you think have high-stakes value. By being proactive in seeking out added responsibilities when you know the work will be redistributed anyway, you also demonstrate engagement and commitment to the company.

Situation 2: Your company is combining divisions and eliminating duplication. How do you demonstrate that you're a stronger candidate to stay than your counterpart?

This is an important time to reflect with an objective eye on your contributions and performance record, especially considering how they can differentiate you from others. It's helpful to show confidence and have the courage to approach your boss to advocate for yourself. Be prepared to describe how your skills and accomplishments apply directly to the strategic needs of the company going forward. Be professional and avoid making any comparisons between you and others who might be vying for positions. This is about you, not them.

Situation 3: You'd just started working for your company when the pandemic sent everyone home to work remotely. You never experienced the natural integration that comes from being around the office. Now everyone is returning. How do you reintroduce yourself and make an impression with people who've met you only on-screen?

Social integration may seem more difficult post-pandemic, but the fundamentals still apply. It doesn't just happen by osmosis. You need to step up. Mention to a colleague you work closely with that you didn't have a chance to be fully introduced to people on the team. Ask them to be an ally and make a point of including you. If you'd like to get to know a particular person better, do what you'd do in any situation—invite them to coffee. Or mention an interest you have in common and use that as a basis for a conversation. In time, shared work projects will create more natural bonds. As a general rule, show by your demeanor and body language that you're interested in others.

Situation 4: There's been a lot of turmoil in your company, and there are rumors that layoffs are coming. But no one is sharing any information. How do you (a) get information about what to expect, or (b) if that doesn't happen, prepare for different possibilities?

You can try to speak to your manager in private and may be received with empathy. However, if this is the climate in your company, you should start preparing to make a move. It has sometimes been said that no answer is an answer. If you're not getting any information or reassurance, read the tea leaves and strategize a plan. This includes networking for new roles, updating your résumé, preparing a financial bridge plan, and framing your mindset to view this change as a new opportunity.

Situation 5: You think working remotely has worked very well and has increased your productivity. Now your boss wants everyone back in the office five days a week. What can you say to advocate for a hybrid situation that allows two to three days at home?

Many organizations started revisiting their remote work policies as soon as the worst of the pandemic was over. If you look at the situation from management's point of view, it's more challenging to manage a team when employees are on different schedules and are rarely in the same office at the same time. If you're feeling pressure from your boss to return to the office, start by understanding where management is coming from. Talk to your boss and ask for his or her reasoning. Are they trying to build a greater team awareness in the office? Are they concerned about productivity and delivering what's needed? Perhaps they're seeing some people fall behind in terms of connectivity, mentoring, or professional development. These are all reasons why an employer may be pushing for teams to be back in the office on a full-time basis. Once you have a sense of the motivations, you can make suggestions that meet those needs but also work for you. For instance, if you commit to being in the office on specific days along with the rest of the team, will that meet the goals of connectivity and alignment? You might also review your goals with your boss and commit to specific deliverables and timing so they feel they can stay on top of your progress in a tangible way. Finally, consider proposing a phasing-in plan for any return to the office, such as being on-site Tuesday through Thursday for six months, and then reviewing. If they're satisfied with your work, they may be willing to make the arrangement permanent.

The Resilience Muscle

"Change moments" that we encounter over the course of our careers allow us to work our resilience muscles. When the rug gets pulled out from under them, people have a tendency to react: "How could this happen to me?" They feel blindsided and even defeated by their unexpectedly shifting environment. But if you think of these change moments as a natural *part* of the environment (which they are!), you'll realize that the key is to develop tools that give you resilience when you encounter them.

Earlier we talked about muscle memory—performing an exercise often enough that your muscles respond without conscious effort—as a way of defining resilience. It works the same way. Every time you encounter a challenge or a stressor, you can perform an action that strengthens your ability to be resilient. Here are some effective ways to build your resilience muscles:

- **Be positive.** In a time of change, pivot to the positive, even if you don't feel it. When there's a change in your environment, ask yourself, *Is there an opportunity here?* Few situations are just plain black-and-white. Try viewing it as a given that you'll be able to find a benefit. Solicit perspectives from others you trust.
- **Nurture commonality.** Continually nurture a sense of common purpose in your workplace. Even if you're not in leadership, you can do this informally through your network and coworkers. Make it a habit to reach out and keep the lines

of communication flowing. When a challenge comes, you'll then have a ready-made support network. Studies show that having a support network encourages a mindset of growth and exploration—just what is needed.

- **Foster "remote" relationships.** We've repeatedly underscored in this book the importance of workplace relationships at all levels. If your workplace has shifted to a hybrid remote/ in person or heavily remote setup, you might feel at a loss about how to foster relationships through a video screen, but it's important for women in particular to figure this out. A study on the effects of remote working shows that the "power of proximity"—the benefit of receiving more feedback while working in person—is most likely to benefit women and younger workers. The catch is that women are most likely to use flexible and remote work options, limiting opportunities for timely performance feedback. Look for ways to build relationships across a variety of channels. Back in the day when our careers involved long-distance relationships with colleagues in other cities or internationally and there was no videoconferencing available, we had to be intentional about our correspondence. Face it—you might never meet some of your colleagues in person. So be creative. Schedule one-on-one video chats or other chances to get more personal. When "remote" colleagues work in the same vicinity, you'll have more options. You just need to make an effort. Reach out and plan face-to-face get-togethers—coffee, a walk, or a small group lunch. People often appreciate the opportunity when someone takes the initiative. Be that person.
- **Embrace change.** Practice stepping outside your comfort zone. In ordinary times when you're not facing an

extraordinary moment, make it a practice to find small ways of mixing it up. Make a change in your daily commute, start a fitness program, pursue a new skill, and so on.

- **Laugh.** Find ways to laugh more, including at yourself. There's no better way to experience common humanity and vulnerability than to share a laugh. According to the Mayo Clinic, there are many short- and long-term benefits of laughter, including increasing release of endorphins and relieving your stress response. In the long run, laughter can strengthen your immune system and increase your happiness.
- **Keep reviewing.** After a major change or challenge, perform an "after-action review." Review what happened, how you handled it, and where you struggled, where systems broke down or could be enhanced, and why. This review will form the basis for creating a better plan for the next time.
- **Take care.** Don't forget self-care. We've talked about self-care in other chapters. The message bears repeating. Especially in a time of change, don't get distracted and neglect your own needs. A little pampering might be called for.

As the song goes, "The fundamental things apply/As time goes by." Being good at what you do, loving your work, wanting to progress in your career—these factors never change no matter the era. The fundamentals still apply. That also holds true for the Career Forward fundamentals we've talked about in this book. Take a moment to review some of the key lessons. They will help you meet any moment, no matter how unexpected. Begin with a commitment to a Career Forward mindset.

Owning the fundamentals will help you remain centered. Imagine that you're going down the river, maneuvering your kayak through rapids. Swing to the right and you could hit rocks. Swing to the left and you could upend the kayak and land in the water. Staying centered means not only keeping your eyes focused ahead but keeping your muscles and your whole body pressed forward.

KEY TAKEAWAYS

- Change is as constant in careers as it is in life.

- An optimistic lens is invaluable. Trials can bring triumphs; change can bring growth.

- Resilience is a valuable professional muscle, and like any muscle, you need to exercise it.

14

It's Worth It

No matter what your ideal work life is, the final goal is the same:
to be able to work with joy.

—Marie Kondo

Think of the Career Forward journey as if it were a rocket launch. At takeoff you rise and try to break free of the atmosphere—and maybe you're shaking like crazy as you reach that point. But then you burst out and you're in orbit. During this process it seems as if the greatest pressure you'll ever experience is during that initial transition. Once you break through the atmosphere, however, it's even harder to stay there. The risk is higher, there's more exposure to the sun. You're constantly fighting gravity, which could pull you down.

The same is true when you achieve a certain level in your career. The higher you rise, the greater your exposure and the more complex your responsibilities and accountability.

You quickly learn that success is not a destination. It's a continuous journey. And with all the work and all the risks, we hope you learn, as we did, that it's worth it. After all, why do astronauts keep fighting to go back into space? Because despite all the stress of putting their lives on the line, they find their fulfillment, their joy, in the endeavor.

We reveled in our careers, rarely feeling as if we were sucking it up for later rewards. Along the way, we built options for an amazing next stage, which we're living now. The Career Forward path offers both pleasure in the ride, and possibilities for the future stages. And here's a key point: your career isn't all about work. It also supports you in finding joy and fulfillment in your personal life. A great career can fund the lifestyle you want to live, help you provide for your loved ones, have a positive impact on others, and leave you with time outside the office. Developing a career that supports you in all these ways isn't easy, but it's worth it.

We're all multidimensional human beings. We're employees, partners, friends, mothers, daughters, granddaughters, sisters, aunts, and more. The pandemic made that clearer than ever, with people's personal life spilling over into their professional life, and vice versa. The sudden change in the professional world made many of us— especially women—reassess our priorities. As we've seen, large numbers of workers chose to part ways with their companies. Hundreds of thousands wondered if they'd *ever* return to the workforce—and for good reason. Many leaders have been worked to the bone. All the long hours at the office and even longer hours traveling all over the globe have made people wonder if their efforts will be worth it in the long run. After all, the pandemic gave the world a poignant reminder that life can be much shorter than we'd hoped.

There are a few ways to look at this situation, and a common one is to see it as a wake-up call to live your best life. But contrary to what many people think, that doesn't mean you should live just for the moment. There's a massive amount of strategy and planning that go into living your best life over the long term, and your career path is a huge part of that.

We wrote this book because we're passionate about helping the women coming up behind us chart their course. We've been very open about the disruptions in the world and workplace that can throw you off-balance. But having the right strategy can make a monumental impact on your outcomes and lead you to a place of fulfillment. The Career Forward mindset we've shared enables you to focus on a long-term view of your career, which will in turn enable you to make the choices that unlock future opportunities, maximize your value, and boost your earning potential.

The Joy of Work

When you consider your career, does it seem separate from the true joy of your life, or is it integrated? Do you ever think, *How much more must I work so I can enjoy the rest of my life?* You'll remember our discussion of the 360-degree perspective, which takes into account your whole self and rejects pitting work against family or pleasure or other aspects of your life. But even when you adopt that perspective, the day-to-day reality of what's in front of you may still not feel like joy.

Joy isn't the same as happiness. It's not a giddy expression or even a big smile or laughter. It's an inner feeling, not always easy to describe. But it shows up in a sense of confidence, a never-ending curiosity, and a deep immersion in the world around you. For example, you might find it hard to picture yourself saying, "I'm so *happy* to be struggling," but how about "This challenge is tough but exhilarating"?

Joy in work is not an elitist idea. It's a fundamental principle of success. Writing in the *Harvard Business Review*, organizational and social psychologist Rebecca Newton, PhD, notes that career growth itself can be a source of joy.[1] She writes: "When I ask my clients about moments in which they experience joy in their work, they tell me about a range of learning experiences, from short but intensive online courses to improve technical skills, being part of management development cohorts that share challenges and ideas, or three-month virtual leadership courses that require hard work on the road to achieving meaningful leadership goals."

Christiana

I left McKinsey after I'd been a senior partner for ten years already. I knew what the job was. I knew what I had to do for my compensation to stay at the level that it was at. I still liked the job, still liked my teams, still liked my clients, but I wasn't challenged. So why did I jump into a corporate role? Because I wanted the challenge; I wanted to continue to develop professionally and personally. Taking on a senior operating role after twenty-four years as a management consultant definitely gave me that opportunity.

Looking back on my whole career, I've been asked whether, if given the choice, I'd do it all over again. People can see things from the outside in, but they don't know what the experience is from the inside out. I've reflected back on how empowering it has been to have this professional identity—to be able to contribute, shape outcomes, be a part of a community, and experience that solidarity. It was fun. And of course it's been satisfying to have financial independence—to be able to provide for my family and have options for where and how to live.

Maybe the biggest justifier of all the effort expended has been discovering my capacities. I've gained enormous confidence. I've built a level of courage I didn't foresee having. And I've developed a phenomenal set of relationships across miles and miles of career. It's staggering when I step back and think about how many people I know that I've worked with and care about.

The Lessons of a Fulfilled Life

Let's step back and consider the key lessons of a fulfilled life from a Career Forward perspective.

Begin by getting crystal clear on what you want out of your personal and professional life, and then use those goals to set personal guardrails for making decisions. Know that what matters most to you is going to be different from what matters most to someone else, so don't let others define what a successful career looks like to you. When you're faced with difficult career decisions, focus on the big picture and know that you're empowered to make the decision that's best for you.

Joy and fulfillment exist within the arena of tough challenges, uncertainties, conflicts, and even misfires. High aspirations, hard work, and personal sacrifice are requirements for a successful career. Don't get comfortable coasting. Instead, always strive to improve yourself so that you can enhance your level of contribution and impact. This, as we've seen, is how you create an opportunity for joy.

People tend not to talk too much about the soaring satisfaction that comes with peak career accomplishments—maybe fearing that it sounds like bragging. But when you reach an important career milestone or knock a project out of the park, be sure to celebrate. Take time to enjoy your achievements. This is a big part of what makes any journey worthwhile and rewarding— actually soaking up the success.

Unexpected changes and opportunities will happen over the course of your career, and you must have the self-awareness needed to recognize such forks in the road. Trust your gut to assess opportunities and be brave. You might just find yourself somewhere you never expected that happens to be the perfect fit.

We think of Carol Tomé, the CEO of UPS, whom Christiana got to know when they both served together on the UPS board of directors. The year after Carol was named CEO of UPS in 2020, she lost her mother. Her sister sent her a photo album with a photo she'd never seen before, and it was a revelation. "It's a picture of four generations—my great-grandmother, my grandmother, my mother, and me, and I'm a baby," she told Atlanta journalist Maria Saporta.[2] "My great-grandmother traveled in a wagon train [and] was a homesteader in Wyoming. My grandmother's husband died when my mother was born. [My grandmother] worked every single day until she died. She walked to work in high heels. She never owned a car. She never owned a home. My mother was a homemaker, who was divorced after twenty-seven years of marriage, took her divorce proceeds and invested them wisely. She'd never had a checkbook. When she passed away, she left a multimillion-dollar estate for her children and grandchildren. And now I'm running UPS, one of the largest companies in the world. I just busted out crying because holy crap, sometimes we think we haven't come very far and we've come so far."

Carol's story of four generations is striking, as is her "holy crap" moment. It's an experience that any woman is capable of having in her career. And the truly remarkable thing about Carol is that the year before she rose to the helm of UPS, she'd retired as chief financial officer at Home Depot after twenty-four years at the company. The new challenge brought her back more energized than ever—right as the world was turning upside down. She sees it as her calling.

No matter your profession or career setting, work to cultivate the entrepreneurial spirit. Neither of us have started a business, but when we've talked to women entrepreneurs, we've noticed a very similar mindset to Career Forward. The very definition of entrepreneurs' jobs is to plunge into the unknown. They revel in it! They don't fear it. It does not occur to them to rely on a safety net. It's empowering to realize that you can have that same spirit no matter what you do.

Grace

I always enjoyed transforming business performance and building new capabilities within companies. I'm not saying every moment was puppies and rainbows, but I loved working in general. Even in the challenging business times, I relished being part of a team and working to solve tough problems. Not only has my career been rewarding and worth it, but it's been enjoyable. Working was also like intellectual food to me as I learned and evolved along the journey. It broadened my worldview and gave me what I thought of as a "full" life.

In the process, it allowed me to be a role model for my children. My kids are independent, hardworking, quality individuals. I felt my career helped me be a good parent. It allowed me to bring more to the table and expose my children to new experiences and ways of thinking. I've been conscious of role modeling a strong work ethic and Career Forward mindset for not only my daughter but my son as they embarked on their separate career journeys.

Be True (and Kind) to Yourself

Success can be addictive, and you may find yourself at the top with a ton of responsibility. Even the best employers may ask "300 percent" of their employees at times. That's why it's essential to have self-awareness. There's a trap inherent in that "300 percent" attitude.

When you put so much hard work and effort into your career, it can feel like everything hinges on driving specific outcomes:

> *"This is a once-in-a-lifetime role!"*
> *"I need this promotion desperately or my résumé will show that I was stagnant for too long!"*

It's good to care deeply about your career and put your best effort forward. But it's also important to maintain perspective. Very few individual events have the power to make or break you. Focusing on achieving perfect outcomes is not realistic, so make sure you self-assess and gauge when you need to take it down a notch. The reality of life is that you do your best, and that's all you can do. You're not in control of everything, and it's important to make peace with that.

We always tell women to remind themselves that no matter what happens, they'll be able to support themselves. When you're a talented hard worker, you'll find opportunities. You need to feel that confidence to take chances and make changes across your career. If things don't go exactly the way you hope, you'll move past the disappointment, and something even better may come along. It can be hard to see in the moment, but difficult times are always balanced with exciting, rewarding times along the way. Make it a priority to perform well and rise to challenges, and you'll enjoy a fulfilling career.

One of the most important lessons we learned over the course of our careers is that sometimes we could have dialed back our intensity. It was our priority to perform well and see how far we could go. We were highly motivated in our careers, but we recognize now that there were plenty of times we could have—and should have—taken a sick day or more personal days to do something fun, or told our bosses that we needed more time to complete a project. In the moment, it seemed like those decisions weren't an option, so we did what was needed and made those sacrifices. But as we think back on those events, they would have been tiny blips on the radar. No one would have held it over our head or thought differently about us if we'd eased back a bit. And being able to cut back would have made it worth it at times.

You can't just keep dialing up the intensity on the treadmill because you're good at it. Develop the skill to know when you should slow down, step off, or speed up.

Gauge your ideal speed by asking the following questions:

- Am I living the life I want to live?
- Are my current efforts helping me get where I want to go?
- Am I regularly doing things to feed my soul?
- Am I fulfilled?

If you answer no to any of these questions, it's time to make a change. See how you can shift your commitments and day-to-day routine to get into a better spot. Know that you're in charge of your life and can cultivate a career that is rewarding and joyful.

When you operate in a mode where full throttle is your standard speed, it will catch up to you. Christiana recalls having a bad cold at one point, and the stress of pushing herself to travel led to a severe ear infection, which in turn became a sinus infection and a double ear infection that grounded her for two weeks. If she'd eased up in the beginning, her recovery would have been quicker. Grace recalls traveling to an international meeting when she had a 101-degree fever.

Once again, the key is looking at the long road. A solid career sets you up to live a happy life. Yes, there will be ups and downs. But the most important thing to remember is that you get only one ticket for this amazing ride, and you should choose to enjoy it.

Christiana

I've had conversations with my son, describing the choices and the sacrifices I've made. For example, I love being close to my family. But that didn't limit my decisions. I moved all the way to New York from college when my entire family was in California. They weren't happy about that, and I missed them, but it was right for me. And I moved to Oregon for Nike when I knew absolutely nobody after I'd had a twenty-four-year career at McKinsey. Everyone was telling me that I should just retire and buy a winery or something—*literally*, they said that, but I was drawn to the possibilities. I kept wanting to "open up more vectors." One of the newest "vectors" for me has been community service—in particular, volunteering with Habitat for Humanity International to create more affordable housing. I began laying the tracks for my involvement with Habitat while I was still working full time, and ultimately I was asked to join the HFHI global board. That's another example of the long-term thinking that comes with a Career Forward mindset—and a 360-degree life.

A sense of adventure and a willingness to pursue your interests, even if they're unconventional, can broaden you. It's a unique mindset, and if it's your path, you'll experience the exhilaration we're talking about.

If you close your eyes and think about how you will look back on your career from the future, you might see all the curves on your road and also the excitement of traveling them. And maybe you'll hear yourself exclaiming, "I can't believe I have this life!"

KEY TAKEAWAYS

- Enjoy the ride.

- Know when to slow down and speed up.

- Challenging times can lead to fulfillment.

- The purpose of striving is the satisfaction and joy you experience.

Acknowledgments

Our greatest opportunities and successes throughout our careers have relied on strong team efforts. That has certainly been true in creating this book. We'd like to thank the team that made it happen: Our agent, Lynn Johnston, believed in us and shepherded our book through the process. She found an excellent home for it at Scribner, and an enthusiastic and insightful editor in Rick Horgan. Rick's contributions have been invaluable. Amelia Forczak and Catherine Whitney were critical partners in helping us shape our ideas and get our thoughts on the page.

We're also grateful to the women leaders who agreed to be interviewed for this book and who shared their important insights and advice: Carrie Cox, Kate Johnson, Pamela Neferkará, Miriam Ort, Shalini Sharp, and Sabrina Simmons.

During her career, Grace has had the blessing of being given opportunities and mentoring from some of the best in business across industries. She appreciates their support, mentoring, sponsorship, and trust. In particular, Grace wants to acknowledge Zein Abdalla, Brian Cornell, Indra Nooyi, Glenn Tilton, Ramon Laguarta, Ronald Schellekens, Hugh Johnston, and Jim Crego.

Christiana has been the grateful recipient of impactful mentoring, honest feedback, caring support, and kicks in the rear from many wonderful colleagues and friends over the years, but there are a few she'd like to call out for special acknowledgement, including:

At McKinsey & Company: Bill Meehan for enrolling her in the "school of Bill" and teaching her how to be a trusted advisor; Nancy Karch for pioneering the retail practice and supporting Christiana in a novel expertise-based career path; and Heidi Raemaekers for keeping Christiana on track and making everything work. Also, Christiana's friends and fellow women senior partners, including Stacey Rauch, Nora Aufreiter, Beth Cobert, and Liz Lempres, for paving dirt roads together and having each other's backs.

At Nike, Inc: Jeanne Jackson for being a constant source of inspiration and mentorship as a client at Banana Republic, a boss at Nike, and ultimately a close friend; Mark Parker for agreeing with Jeanne that bringing a longtime consultant into a senior operating role at Nike was a good idea; Trevor Edwards for challenging Christiana and her teams to go further, faster, better; and Erin Longmate for going above and beyond to support Christiana at Nike and ever since.

And finally, across Christiana's family: a special shout-out to her daughter-in-law, Alyson, and all of Christiana's nieces for sharing their career journeys, asking for Christiana's advice, and giving feedback on whether it was helpful. The first beta testers for Career Forward!

In conclusion, we both want to acknowledge the young women coming up who aspire to be leaders and break new ground. This book is both our gift to them and a tribute to the new possibilities we know they'll create.

Notes

INTRODUCTION: AT THE TOP OF YOUR GAME

1. Rachel Muller-Heyndyk, "Women Work Harder but Progress Less at Work," HR magazine, April 2, 2019, https://www.hrmagazine.co.uk /content/news/women-work-harder-but-progress-less-at-work/.

CHAPTER 1: WE HAVE SOMETHING TO TELL YOU

1. Alexandra Olson and the Associated Press, "Women Hold a Record Number of Corporate Board Seats. The Bad News: It's Barely Over 25%, and It's Slowing Down," *Fortune*, September 30, 2022, https://fortune.com/2022/09/30/how -many-women-sit-corporate-boards-record-28-percent-russell-3000/.
2. Alicia Adamczyk, "Americans Are in the Era of Quiet Ambition: No Longer 'Chasing Achievement for Achievement's Sake,'" *Fortune*, April 16, 2023, https://fortune.com/2023/04/16/americans-enter-quiet-ambition-era/.
3. *Women in America: Work and Life Well-Lived*, Gallup, 2016 report, https:// www.gallup.com/workplace/238070/women-america-work-life-lived -insights-business-leaders.aspx.

CHAPTER 2: CAREER FORWARD

1. Paulina Cachero, "Most U.S. College Grads Don't Work in the Field They Studied, Survey Finds," Bloomberg, April 18, 2022, https://www.bloomberg .com/news/articles/2022-04-18/is-college-worth-it-most-graduates-work-in -other-fields#xj4y7vzkg.
2. Jackie Swift, "The Benefits of Having a Sense of Purpose," Research & Innovation, Cornell University, https://research.cornell.edu/news-features /benefits-having-sense-purpose.

CHAPTER 3: GROW YOUR PROFESSIONAL EQUITY

1. Rocío Lorenzo, Nicole Voigt, Miki Tsusaka, Matt Krentz, and Kate Abou- zahr, "How Diverse Leadership Teams Boost Innovation," BCG

.com, January 23, 2018, https://www.bcg.com/publications/2018/how
-diverse-leadership-teams-boost-innovation.

2. Vivian Hunt, Lareina Yee, Sara Prince, and Sundiatu Dixon-Fyle,
"Delivering Through Diversity," McKinsey & Company, January 18, 2018,
https://www.mckinsey.com/capabilities/people-and-organizational
-performance/our-insights/delivering-through-diversity.

3. Vivian Hunt, Sundiatu Dixon-Fyle, Sara Prince, and Kevin Dolan,
"Diversity Wins: How Inclusion Matters," McKinsey & Company, May 19,
2020, https://www.mckinsey.com/~/media/mckinsey/featured%20insights
/diversity%20and%20inclusion/diversity%20wins%20how%20inclusion
%20matters/diversity-wins-how-inclusion-matters-vf.pdf.

4. Erik Larson, "New Research: Diversity + Inclusion = Better Decision
Making," *Forbes*, September 21, 2017, https://www.forbes.com/sites/eriklarson
/2017/09/21/new-research-diversity-inclusion-better-decision-making
-at-work/?sh=40c7e51c4cbf.

5. Rocío Lorenzo and Martin Reeves, "How and Where Diversity Drives
Financial Performance," *Harvard Business Review*, January 30, 2018, https://
hbr.org/2018/01/how-and-where-diversity-drives-financial-performance.

6. Christie Smith and Stephanie Turner, PhD, "The Radical Transformation
of Diversity & Inclusion: The Millennial Influence," Deloitte University
Leadership Center for Inclusion, https://www2.deloitte.com/content
/dam/Deloitte/us/Documents/about-deloitte/us-inclus-millennial
-influence-120215.pdf.

CHAPTER 4: GET FULL VALUE

1. Charlotte Klein and Julie Ma, "How to Negotiate a Salary, According to
25 Famous Women," The Cut, *New York*, September 23, 2020, https://www
.thecut.com/2020/09/25-famous-women-on-how-to-negotiate-salary.html.

2. Carolina Aragão, "Gender Pay Gap in U.S. Hasn't Changed Much in Two
Decades," Pew Research Center, March 1, 2023, https://www.pewresearch
.org/short-reads/2023/03/01/gender-pay-gap-facts/.

3. Kim Elsesser, "Unequal Pay, Unconscious Bias, and What to Do About It,"
Forbes, April 10, 2018, https://www.forbes.com/sites/kimelsesser
/2018/04/10/unequal-pay-unconscious-bias-and-what-to-do-about-it
/?sh=2ebd7a1c600e.

4. Elise Gould, Jessica Schieder, and Kathleen Geier, "What Is the Gender Pay
Gap and Is It Real?" Economic Policy Institute, October 20, 2016, https://
www.epi.org/publication/what-is-the-gender-pay-gap-and-is-it-real/.

CHAPTER 5: THE UNDERDOG'S SUPERPOWER

1. LeanIn.org and McKinsey & Company, "Women in the Workplace 2022,"
October 18, 2022, https://leanin.org/women-in-the-workplace/2022.

2. "Women in the Workplace 2022." https://www.mckinsey.com/featured
-insights/diversity-and-inclusion/women-in-the-workplace.

3. Shelley Correll, *Creating a Level Playing Field* (video), Clayman Institute for Gender Research, Stanford University, https://www.youtube.com/watch?v=YPoymWLNjVk.
4. Kelly Shue, "Women Aren't Promoted Because Managers Underestimate Their Potential," Yale Insights, September 17, 2021, https://insights.som.yale.edu/insights/women-arent-promoted-because-managers-underestimate-their-potential.
5. *What Is Performance Bias?* (video), LeanIn, https://leanin.org/education/what-is-performance-bias.
6. Skip Prichard, "A Conversation with Condoleezza Rice," December 15, 2011, https://www.skipprichard.com/conversation-condoleezza-rice/.
7. Patrick Reed, "How Our Brains Are Biologically Tuned to Be Influenced by Confident People," University of Sussex, December 13, 2016; Dr. Daniel Campbell-Meiklejohn, Arndis Simonsen, Chris D. Frith, and Nathaniel D. Daw, "Independent Neural Computation of Value from Other People's Confidence," *Journal of Neuroscience* 37, no. 3 (2017): 673–84.
8 Piercarlo Valdesolo, "Bet on the Losing Team," *Scientific American*, June 28, 2011, https://www.scientificamerican.com/article/bet-on-the-losing-team/.
9. Samir Nurmohamed, "The Upside of Being an Underdog," *Harvard Business Review*, January 14, 2020, https://hbr.org/2020/01/the-upside-of-being-an-underdog.

CHAPTER 8: YOUR 360-DEGREE LIFE
1. LeanIn.org and McKinsey & Company, "Women in the Workplace 2022," October 18, 2022, https://leanin.org/women-in-the-workplace/2022.
2. Chris Kolmar, "25+ Telling Paternity Leave Statistics [2023]: Average Paternity Leave Length," Zippia, June 22, 2023, https://www.zippia.com/advice/paternity-leave-statistics/; U.S. Bureau of Labor Statistics, https://www.bls.gov/ebs/factsheets/family-leave-benefits-fact-sheet.htm.
3. "Women in the Workplace 2022."
4. Emma Hinchliffe and Kinsey Crowley, "This CEO Thought She Understood the Reality of Caregiving for Employees—Until She Became a Caregiver Herself," The Broadsheet, *Fortune*, January 26, 2023, https://fortune.com/2023/01/26/this-ceo-thought-she-understood-the-reality-of-caregiving-for-employees-until-she-became-a-caregiver-herself/.
5. "Women in the Workplace 2022."

CHAPTER 9: LUCKY LIKE A DUCK
1. Aman Kidwai, "Getting More Black Women on Corporate Boards Is This Program's Urgent Mission," *Fortune*, February 1, 2022, https://fortune.com/2022/02/01/black-women-on-boards-representation-executives-diversity/.

CHAPTER 10: FACING THE FORKS IN THE ROAD

1. Marc Effron and Miriam Ort, *One Page Talent Management: Eliminating Complexity, Adding Value* (Cambridge, MA: Harvard Business Review Press, 2010).

CHAPTER 11: SHAPING YOUR LEADERSHIP IDENTITY

1. "Will Teen Girls Close the Gender Gap?" Harvard Graduate School of Education, July 28, 2015, https://www.gse.harvard.edu/news/15/07/will -teen-girls-close-gender-gap.
2. Always #LikeAGirl campaign, https://www.always.com/en-us/about-us /our-epic-battle-like-a-girl.
3. Jack Zenger and Joseph Folkman, "Research: Women Are Better Leaders During a Crisis," *Harvard Business Review*, December 30, 2020, https://hbr .org/2020/12/research-women-are-better-leaders-during-a-crisis.
4. Emma Hinchliffe and Kinsey Crowley, "Bed Bath & Beyond CEO Is the Latest Example of a Female Leader Facing a 'Glass Cliff,'" The Broadsheet, *Fortune*, April 26, 2023, https://fortune.com/2023/04/26/bed-bath-beyond -ceo-sue-gove-glass-cliff/.
5. Avivah Wittenberg-Cox, "Data Shows Women Make Better Leaders. Who Cares?" *Forbes*, March 6, 2021, https://www.forbes.com/sites/avivahwitten bergcox/2021/03/06/data-shows-women-make-better-leaders-whocares /?sh=29b68b3346be.
6. Carol S. Dweck, *Mindset: The New Psychology of Success* (New York: Random House, 2006).
7. Bryan Stevenson, *Just Mercy: A Story of Justice and Redemption* (New York: Spiegel & Grau), 2014.
8. Jennifer Aaker and Naomi Bagdonas, *Humor, Seriously: Why Humor Is a Secret Weapon in Business and Life* (New York: Currency, 2021).
9. Ella Miron-Spektor, Julia Bear, Emuna Eliav, Li Huang, Melanie Milovac, and Eric Yuge Lou, "Research: Being Funny Can Pay Off More for Women Than Men," *Harvard Business Review*, April 14, 2023, https://hbr.org/2023/04 /research-being-funny-can-pay-off-more-for-women-than-men.

CHAPTER 12: OWN YOUR AMBITION

1. Marguerite Ward, "Women Are Afraid to Call Themselves 'Ambitious' at Work and It's Seriously Hurting Their Careers," *Business Insider*, March 8, 2020, https://www.businessinsider.com/psychologist-recommend-strategies -ambition-women-at-work-career-goals.
2. Liz Elting, "The High Cost of Ambition: Why Women Are Held Back for Thinking Big," *Forbes*, April 24, 2017, https://www.forbes.com/sites /lizelting/2017/04/24/the-high-cost-of-ambition-why-women-are-held -back-for-thinking-big/?sh=1a7931251ee6.
3. Katie Abouzahr, Matt Krentz, Claire Tracey, and Miki Tsusaka, "Dispelling the Myths of the Gender 'Ambition Gap,'" BCG, April 5, 2017,

https://www.bcg.com/publications/2017/people-organization-leadership
-change-dispelling-the-myths-of-the-gender-ambition-gap.

4. Tory Burch, "Don't Wait for Doors to Open," LinkedIn, April 21, 2016,
https://www.linkedin.com/pulse/dont-wait-doors-open-tory-burch/?trk=li
_fb_namer_mmc_ToryBurch_Facebook_mm&utm_campaign=Tory-
Burch&utm_medium=social&utm_source=Facebook&utm_content=mm.

5. David Shindler, "Are Women More Collaborative and Men More
Competitive?" LinkedIn, October 2, 2018, https://www.linkedin.com
/pulse/women-more-collaborative-men-competitive-david-shindler/.

6. Judith Warner and Danielle Corley, "The Women's Leadership Gap,"
Center for American Progress, November 20, 2018, https://www.american
progress.org/article/womens-leadership-gap-2/.

CHAPTER 13: MEET THE MOMENT

1. Chris Bradley, Martin Hirt, Sara Hudson, Nicholas Northcote, and Sven Smit,
"The Great Acceleration," McKinsey & Company, July 14, 2020, https://www
.mckinsey.com/capabilities/strategy-and-corporate-finance/our-insights
/the-great-acceleration; Kevin Sneader and Shubham Singhal, "The Next
Normal Arrives: Trends That Will Define 2021—and Beyond," McKinsey &
Company, January 4, 2021, https://www.mckinsey.com/featured-insights
/leadership/the-next-normal-arrives-trends-that-will-define-2021-and-beyond.

2. Kim Parker and Juliana Menasce Horowitz, "Majority of Workers Who
Quit a Job in 2021 Cite Low Pay, No Opportunity for Advancement, Feeling
Disrespected," Pew Research Center, March 9, 2022, https://www.pew
research.org/short-reads/2022/03/09/majority-of-workers-who-quit-a-job-in
-2021-cite-low-pay-no-opportunities-for-advancement-feeling-disrespected/.

3. Taylor Telford, "Quiet Quitting Isn't Really About Quitting. Here Are the
Signs," *Washington Post*, August 21, 2022, https://www.washingtonpost.com
/business/2022/08/21/quiet-quitting-what-to-know/#.

4. Aditya Malik, "Quiet Hiring: A New Workplace Trend for Companies,"
Forbes, April 18, 2023, https://www.forbes.com/sites/forbestechcouncil
/2023/04/18/quiet-hiring-a-new-workplace-trend-for-companies/?sh
=537d43342f32.

CHAPTER 14: IT'S WORTH IT

1. Rebecca Newton, "Rediscover Joy at Work," *Harvard Business Review*,
September 8, 2021, https://hbr.org/2021/09/rediscover-joy-at-work.

2. Maria Saporta, "Carol Tomé on Becoming CEO of UPS: 'This Was My
Calling,'" Saporta Report, March 8, 2021, https://saportareport.com
/carol-tome-on-becoming-ceo-of-ups-this-was-my-calling/columnists
/maria_saporta/.

INDEX